PROCUREMENT POLICY, STRATEGY AND PROCEDURES

SPIRO BUSINESS GUIDES

Spiro Business Guides are designed to provide managers with practical, down-to-earth information, and they are written by leading authors in their respective fields. If you would like to receive a full listing of current and forthcoming titles, please visit www.spiropress.com or email spiropress@capita-ld.co.uk or call us on +44 (0)870 400 1000.

PROCUREMENT POLICY, STRATEGY AND PROCEDURES

A PRACTICAL GUIDE

STEPHEN CANNON

First published in 2005 by
Spiro Press
17–19 Rochester Row
London
SW1P 1LA
Telephone: +44 (0)870 400 1000

© Stephen Cannon, 2005

ISBN: 1 84439 066 7

British Library Cataloguing-in-Publication Data.
A catalogue record for this book is available from the British Library.

Disclaimer: This publication is intended to assist you in identifying issues which you should know about and about which you may need to seek specific advice. It is not intended to be an exhaustive statement of the law or a substitute for seeking specific advice.

Stephen Cannon asserts his moral right to be identified as the author of this work.

Spiro Press USA
3 Front Street, Suite 331
PO Box 338
Rollinsford
NH 03869
USA

Printed and bound in Great Britain by: Digital Book Logistics
Cover design by: REAL451
Cover typeset by: The Composing Room

Spiro Press is part of The Capita Group Plc

To Shelagh, Christopher, Paul and Philip

Contents

List of figures and tables

Figures

Tables

Introduction

The book should help two types of reader, namely:

- professional procurement practitioners; and

- non-practitioners, who might be internal customers or senior management.

For the procurement practitioner, the book should help to develop a policy, a strategy and a set of procedures from scratch. The contents are based on the temPLATES offered by Knowledge Aware Limited. While these temPLATES will undoubtedly shorten the time needed to arrive at finished documents, it should be possible for a practitioner to produce a sound set of procurement documents simply by following this book providing he or she has the time and good drafting skills.

For non-procurement practitioners, particularly those in senior management, this book should be regarded as a guide to how procurement should be conducted. It should help to benchmark the processes which are needed for procurement to add value to the bottom line of the organisation while simultaneously protecting it from ethical, commercial and contractual failures.

The differences in organisational structures and the degree to which purchasing is centralised or decentralised mean that the suggestions in the book will need to be adapted to the reader's organisation. The book has been written with this very much in mind and the importance of organisational structure or procurement and its effect on producing and implementing a procurement policy, strategy and set of procedures is discussed.

The book has been written in the United Kingdom and, occasionally, it makes reference to that country. However, these are not extensive and readers from other countries will hopefully not be discouraged by them. It should be perfectly possible for a person of another nationality to mentally substitute a reference to his or her own country's law or culture and to use the content of these pages.

Acknowledgements

Chapter 13 has been reviewed by Philip Hong of AMEX and Max Chatterjee of MasterCard. Many thanks to both for all their help.

About the author

Stephen Cannon is a professional procurement practitioner who has worked in procurement at all management levels ranging from the tactical to the strategic. He has written widely about procurement. He has developed training programmes and products for procurement, such as the Certification Product of the Chartered Institute of Purchasing and Supply and Knowledge Aware's Contract Law INFOcharts. He was the first person to draw attention to the need for marketing procurement to internal customers when he wrote a series of articles about this subject in the precursor to the Chartered Institute's bi-monthly magazine.

The author may be contacted via the publishers.

CHAPTER 1

Procurement policy, strategy and procedures – the whys and wherefores

Definitions of policy, strategy and procedures

- *Policy* – a course of action or set of principles described at a high level which apply to an individual or an organisation.

- *Strategy* – a plan intended to put a long-term aim, such as a policy, into effect.

- *Procedure* – an instruction or a description of how something should be done.

Corporate procurement policy – relationship with corporate objectives

The objective of a corporate procurement policy is to list what principles or courses of action will underpin the organisation's procurement. These corporate procurement principles and courses of action need to be compatible with the policies and objectives which govern the overall corporate approach to its business (see Figure 1.1).

In the private sector, an organisation's business objectives might be market growth or increasing profitability through a variety of means. In the public sector, the objectives might be providing more public sector services at reduced/contained cost or even at reasonable cost to the tax payer. Organisations, whether private or public sector, should also have policies and objectives about issues such as the environment, health and safety and fair trade. In many countries issues of this sort are the subject of legislation and, if this is the case, their application to procurement could be essential to avoid the organisation falling foul of the law.

The reason for having a corporate procurement policy is to make sure that procurement plays its full role in contributing to the overall business objectives in a way which is compatible with the principles and the societal and legal concerns of the organisation.

Who undertakes procurement and how procurement is structured in an organisation has a major bearing on corporate procurement policy development. In only a few organisations is procurement a major function standing alongside and on equal terms with other major service functions such as HR, marketing or finance.

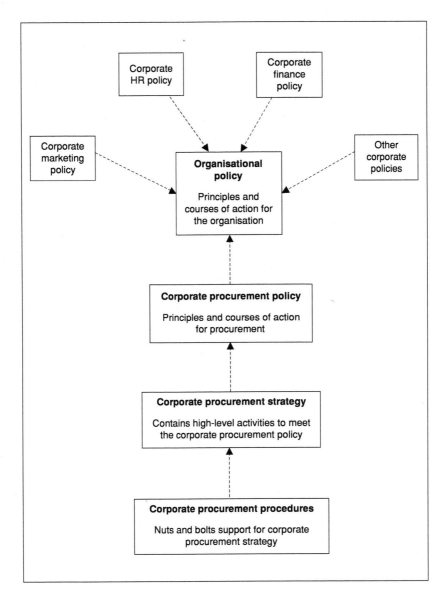

Figure 1.1 Relationships between corporate procurement policy, strategy and procedures and organisational policy.

Corporate procurement strategy – what it is

The definition of strategy refers to a plan. A plan is a list of activities to be carried out to achieve a long-term aim, such as a policy. Strategies should be high level, leaving tactics to deal with the detail. Corporate procurement strategies describe the activities needed to meet the corporate procurement policy as well as the objectives and goals of the organisation.

The corporate procurement strategy should not go into the detailed 'nuts and bolts'. These are best left to the procedures. For procurement, the strategy acts as the bridge between the policy and the procedures (see Figure 1.2). Its prepares the ground for the procedures. Usually, it will be easier to get senior management in an organisation to take an interest in the corporate procurement strategy than in the corporate procurement procedures. We discuss this below.

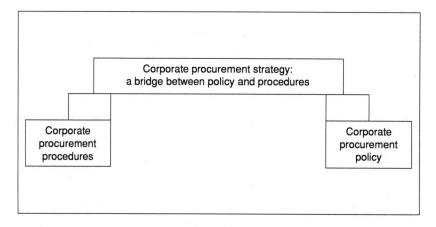

Figure 1.2 Relationships between corporate procurement policy, strategy and procedures.

Corporate procurement procedures

The dictionary definition of procedures is particularly apt for corporate procurement procedures. They are usually a set of statements about a preferred approach which is often mandatory for all those engaged in procurement in the organisation.

Procedures try to standardise and explain tasks so that the individual is not required to constantly reinvent the wheel. The objective is to make processes more efficient by identifying the best, recording it and then applying it to future similar circumstances. This provides an opportunity to simplify processes and reduce waste.

However, there are some problems with standardising on one preferred procedural approach. Circumstances are not always exact repetitions of one another, so procedures are not always apt and a reduction of discretion can mean a reduction in the job interest for the individuals doing the work. In fact, written procedures can be unpopular particularly if they stifle innovation and initiative. To simplify processes and reduce waste, they need to be prescriptive, but not to the extent that they stifle the individual.

Corporate procurement procedures: key objectives

Good procedures, whether for procurement or any other discipline, should help realise several key objectives (see Figure 1.3).

1. *Saving of time by not reinventing the wheel*

2. *Management and measurement of processes*

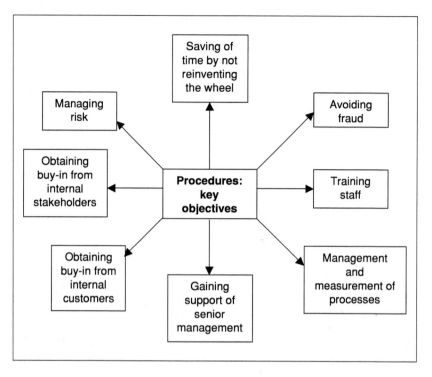

Figure 1.3 Corporate procedures: key objectives.

3. Training staff

Procedures are obviously helpful to new and existing staff as they instruct them about how things should be done in the organisation. For procedures to be successful forms of instruction, they have to be written in a readable style but it helps a lot if they can be supplemented by some form of instruction. Few organisations devote much time to training personnel about the content of their procurement procedures – they assume that the written word is enough. However, short sessions to discuss procedures can be an excellent way of cementing their use by persuading individuals of the need for them. Such sessions can also be an opportunity for individuals to explore the practicality of the procedures by checking when they work and when they do not and identifying when they should be revised. In this way, all individuals feel they are a part of the process of writing procedures. This makes people something more than just cogs in their application.

4. Avoiding fraud

Procedures are a way of avoiding fraud. They should require an audit trail and they define processes which will make fraud more difficult. The incidence of fraud in organisations is known to be large but nobody (not surprisingly) knows how large. Many organisations prefer not to publicise those occasions when they discover fraud because of the embarrassment which the publicity would cause. Procurement is one of those areas where poor management can make fraud a strong possibility. Good procedures can help an organisation prevent fraudulent activity.

5. Gaining support of senior management

Corporate procurement procedures should preferably be championed and endorsed by the CEO or the organisation's main board as this gives them credibility. Gaining that endorsement provides another opportunity for marketing procurement to the senior management of the organisation.

Careful thought needs to be given to how senior management can be given an understanding of the content of the procedures. It is very unlikely that they will want to read them, so a digest of some sort will be needed.

6. Obtaining buy-in from internal customers

By internal customers we mean those for whom the procurement operation is providing a service. Involving internal customers in the drafting of the procedures is also a way of giving the procedures a stamp of approval. Some internal customers will want to play an active role in developing the procedures. They will need to understand why procedures are needed and be involved in their selection and development. Some internal customers may be anxious that their role in the procurement will be terminated. They might be encouraged if they realise that good procurement is usually a team effort and that the procedures will reflect this aspiration.

Their degree of involvement needs to be carefully thought through. Having them involved should aid acceptance and credibility. However, having too many involved can slow the whole process down.

Some internal customers may have no wish to be involved but that does not mean that they should not be kept informed. This can be best done by briefings at regular intervals culminating in a digest which, depending on circumstances, might be similar to the one used for senior management.

This digest will need to clearly state what the impact on the internal customer will be when the procedures are put into effect. Giving the internal customers an incorrect impression of the amount of work or involvement in procurement which will fall to them after the procedures have been implemented can be very disillusioning.

There will also probably be internal customers who would like to be involved but should not be. Some tact will be required to cope with this problem.

7. Obtaining buy-in from internal stakeholders

Obvious examples are the finance, audit and legal departments. These departments need to be involved, or at least kept informed. They usually have a lot of influence about how things should be done and it would be unfortunate if their influence were exerted adversely after the procedures had been completed.

8. Managing risk

Good procedures assist in the management of both legal and commercial risk.

While there is no legal requirement for an organisation to have corporate procurement procedures, there are various legal requirements with which organisations must comply when undertaking their procurement. For example, for utilities and for the public sector in the European Union, there are the various rules laid down in the European Procurement Directives which define how they should conduct many aspects of their procurement. Similar rules apply to public sector organisations in many other countries. Obviously, the corporate procurement procedures must take account of these. All organisations should take account in their procurement procedures of late payment legislation, health and safety legislation, etc. where such legislation exists.

With respect to commercial risk, the objective of the procedures is to ensure that the processes which are followed will keep commercial risk to a minimum while maintaining a reasonable balance of risk between the supplier and the procurement organisation.

Early steps for consideration

At an early stage when considering the development of corporate procurement policy, strategy and procedures, it helps to think through the following:

- Which internal customers need to be involved?

- Which internal customers would like to be involved and can their wishes be accommodated?

- Who would prefer a less involved role but their endorsement is needed? In such a case the briefing and digest approach, mentioned above, could be helpful.

- Which internal stakeholders need to be involved and how they should be involved?

- Who will produce the digest for senior management and, if required, for internal customers and what should it contain?

- Who will do the drafting of the policy, strategy and procedures? It will need to be somebody with good drafting skills.

- Who will research and select from alternative approaches if such exist? This might not be the same person as the one doing the drafting.

- Who needs to be involved from inside procurement? This obviously depends on how procurement is managed in the organisation. This is discussed in Chapter 2.

- How will senior management approval be gained? Will a digest be necessary?

- What will be the final format of the documents?

- How they will be disseminated?

- What training should accompany them?

CHAPTER 2

Procurement and organisational objectives and structures

As previously mentioned, procurement must contribute to the business objectives of the organisation. In the private sector, business objectives tend to centre on growing market share, increasing profits and protecting the company. In the public sector, the objective is to serve the citizen better within a budget.

In many organisations, the main expectation of the management of the organisation and the procurement professionals themselves is to find savings, whether these are price or cost reductions or avoidance of price or cost increases.

This emphasis on savings as an objective of professionally conducted procurement is not unreasonable but it should not be exclusive. Well managed procurement has much more to offer organisations in the achievement of their goals and the next two sections of this chapter illustrate this. It is important that a procurement policy and a procurement strategy define procurement's contribution to the organisation in terms of the total value which it can add and not just in terms of the savings which it can realise.

Procurement's value-add to private sector organisational goals

Organisations in the private sector often have the following objectives:

- improving the sales performance of existing products in existing markets;

- selling into new markets;

- eliminating underperforming products;

- developing and launching new products for the existing markets;

- developing and launching new products for new markets;

- acquisition of new businesses or products for existing markets;

- acquisition of new businesses or products for new markets;

- merging with competitors, suppliers or customers;

- focus on core activities with divestment of non-core activities which can include products;

- more stringent cost control.

Good procurement can contribute by adding value to all of the above goals as Table 2.1 illustrates.

Table 2.1 Contribution by good procurement

Private sector organisation strategy	Corporate procurement strategy
Improving the performance of existing products in the marketplace	• Speed up delivery • Reduce cost • Increase features at no or low extra cost • Improve quality • Increase capacity at existing suppliers
Selling into new markets	• Find new effective sources of supply local to the new market • Renegotiate existing contracts to make them compatible with selling into new markets • Arrange delivery to new markets • Adjust the product specification to meet more exactly the needs of the new market • Increase capacity at existing suppliers

Private sector organisation strategy	Corporate procurement strategy
Eliminating underperforming products	• Negotiate and manage the early termination of contracts with suppliers
Developing and launching new products for the existing markets	• Find new, effective suppliers of goods and services not hitherto purchased • Let new business to existing suppliers • Develop contracts to meet the business need
Developing and launching new products for new markets	• Find new, effective suppliers of goods and services not hitherto purchased • Manage the supplier involvement in product development • Let new business to existing suppliers • Develop contracts to meet the business need
Acquisition of new businesses or products for existing markets	• Identifying the procurement overlap between the old business (or products) and the new business (or products) and manage the elimination

Private sector organisation strategy	Corporate procurement strategy
	of the overlap which might involve early termination of contracts, increasing capacity at selected suppliers, etc.
Merging with competitors, suppliers or customers	• Identify and manage the elimination of any procurement overlap • Amalgamate and/or standardise procurement systems • Ensure existing contracts are managed effectively until their expiry/ termination
Focus on core activities with divestment of non-core activities which can include products	• Take steps to ensure the transfer of supplier relationships and the associated contracts to other organisations • Develop contracts to facilitate the transfer of the divested activities • If the divestment is outsourcing, find suppliers which can effectively and efficiently supply the divested services

Private sector organisation strategy	Corporate procurement strategy
More stringent cost control	• Find savings • Streamline processes, for example by the introduction of purchase cards and the use of e-procurement and other IT techniques

Procurement's value-add to public sector organisational goals

Procurement can also add value to public sector goals.

The public sector achieves its objectives in the following sorts of ways:

- outsourcing activities via Private Finance Initiatives (PFIs), Public Private Partnerships (PPPs) and privatisation;

- improving service delivery to the citizen by the introduction of new ways of doing things or by doing existing things better – examples include improved medical techniques, new computer systems to give swifter responses to the citizen;

- insourcing – for example the effective insourcing of the rail network in the UK and the insourcing of contracts associated with the maintenance of that network;

- restructuring of public sector bodies;

- establishing new public sector bodies;

- public sector initiatives to improve themselves (for example, the Best Value approach to local government in the UK);

- public sector audits and investigations;

- cost reduction.

Table 2.2 maps possible procurement value-add to these objectives.

Table 2.2 Contribution to public sector objectives

Public sector organisation strategy	Corporate procurement strategy
Outsourcing activities via PFI, PPP and privatisation	• Identify suppliers • Develop appropriate contracts and contract strategies
Improving service delivery to the citizen by the introduction of new ways of doing things or by doing existing things better	• Streamline procurement processes • Review markets to find new ideas and suppliers of improved processes • Manage the supply of all goods and services needed to support the improved ways of doing things

Public sector organisation strategy	Corporate procurement strategy
Insourcing – for example, insourcing the maintenance contracts for the UK rail network	• Deal with the contracts affected by insourcing such as those let with suppliers prior to insourcing • Let new contracts if needed to support the insourcing
Restructuring of public sector bodies	• Manage the contracts with suppliers if those contracts are affected by the restructuring
Establishing new public sector bodies	• Establish an effective procurement platform to support the new public sector body
Public sector initiatives to improve themselves, for example Best Value in local government in the UK	• Participating in the initiative by challenging existing ways of doing things and developing new sources of supply to support any new approaches
Public sector audits and investigations	• Ensure sound audit trails exist
Cost reduction	• Supply side cost reduction

Note

Neither the corporate strategies nor the corporate procurement strategies given in Tables 2.1 and 2.2 are intended to be an exhaustive list. They illustrate a possible range of corporate strategies and a supporting procurement strategy which is often more than making savings.

Organisational structures for procurement

The extent to which a procurement department can make a fully strategic contribution to corporate goals depends on the position of professional procurement in the organisation. Position is a combination of the structure of procurement in the organisation and the extent to which the senior management and procurement's internal customers consider that it makes a valuable contribution to the organisation.

There are three possible organisational structures for procurement:

- decentralised;

- centralised;

- centralised/decentralised (also known as CLAN, or centre-led action network).

Organisations can go through all of these structures as a cycle and, to understand this, it can be helpful to consider how procurement develops as an activity in an organisation.

When an entrepreneur begins a new business, procurement is one of the things which the entrepreneur does. Finding customers and making sales is the prime concern of a new enterprise and, unless the business is in the retail or wholesaling sectors, procurement is a function but it might not be a business critical one.

Even in new organisations, which sell what they buy (possibly after some form of processing), where it might be expected that procurement is an important contributor to sales, most entrepreneurs want sales rather than savings. The focus is probably on marketing, sales, production, finance and administration in that order. Procurement might be no more than an administrative chore. At this stage, procurement is centralised.

As the organisation grows, it recruits more staff – most probably the initial recruitment will be in operations and sales, then in marketing, finance and HR. Procurement tends to become more dispersed to the personnel in these functions, particularly if the procurement is to satisfy the business needs of those staff, for example their needs for IT equipment and software, travel, transport, office equipment, etc. It is quite possible that business-critical procurement will still be undertaken by the entrepreneur but it will be one of many tasks and not necessarily given the attention which it deserves. At this stage, procurement is becoming increasingly decentralised.

Professional procurement tends to come into its own in medium/large organisations whose procurement has not changed from their growth phase. That is to say, procurement might be widely dispersed and undertaken by many in the organisation, often buying the same things at very different prices on various terms and conditions from a number of different suppliers. It might still be the original entrepreneur, if he or she is still around, who does the business-critical procurement, cramming it into a busy schedule or arbitrarily delegating it.

This is the reason why it is relatively easy to go into such businesses and identify savings. It is because procurement has not previously been identified as a significant business function requiring full-time expertise. The business was too busy growing and/or surviving for its personnel to attend to it properly.

Professional procurement is often brought into organisations after financial difficulty and sometimes on the coat-tails of consultants. The usual reaction to financial difficulty is to cut costs. Advertising, training and recruitment are often the first to go, followed by manpower and then by an attack on procurement costs. The approach is normally to consolidate and leverage spends. This means identifying market segments which can supply a range of goods or services and leveraging the spend, usually by reducing the number of suppliers (supplier base reduction).

In addition, processes are streamlined and genuine low-value low-risk procurement is left at the user/internal customer level. Procurement becomes a service function in that it provides cost reductions to the organisation (often when it most needs it) and a procurement service by supplying the right goods and services of the right quality at the right time at the right cost to the right place (the so-called 'five rights').

The structure of procurement at this stage is centralised. Strong senior management support is usually needed to compel the decentralised structure to release the procurement to the

---

centre. If this support is not forthcoming in any consistent way, there will be a 'purchasing tug of war' between the centralised procurement unit and those members of staff who have been doing the procurement hitherto. Sometimes, those members of staff never surrender their procurement activities. It is this tug of war which is ultimately the source of professional procurement's complaints about 'maverick purchasing', that is internal customers still doing their own procurement and disregarding the centrally let procurement contracts.

If business critical procurement is still being undertaken more or less exclusively by the original entrepreneur or his or her successors, they need to be persuaded to relinquish their grip. This can be difficult. It is not unknown for entrepreneurs to call in the professionals to advise and then to resent the advice, particularly if it implies criticism of the entrepreneur him or herself!

Leveraging spends is not something which can be continued indefinitely. A base is reached even though this can be extended by using value engineering techniques and partnering relationships, assuming suppliers are willing to cooperate. Ultimately, savings are less easy to find except on an ad hoc basis, which is one of the reasons why non-professionals can, on occasions, find better deals than the professional. It is also true that centralised structures can over a period of time become rather remote and self-interested. They are usually not ideally placed to move procurement into its more strategic role of identifying with other aspects of corporate strategy than cost reduction. A change of structure is needed and the most appropriate is some form of centralised/decentralised structure.

In this model, procurement of any category is conducted by individuals dispersed to the business units which have the major need for that category of goods or services. There is a centre which provides guidance and advice, and which addresses strategic issues and works with the senior management in the organisation to do so. The centre's role includes the measurement of performance and development of process.

The above model (illustrated in Figure 2.1) goes some way to help describe and understand the structures which develop. However, in the real business world, things often have a habit of refusing to conform to models. Any model is a good representation but there are always exceptions.

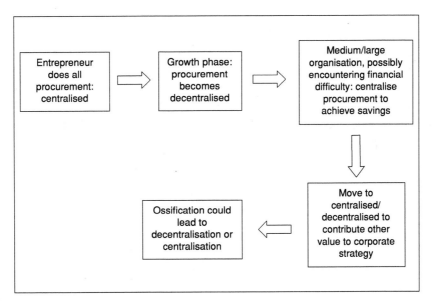

Figure 2.1 Development of the procurement function.

All business structures ossify after a period of time, possibly because those who work in them become too comfortable and too concerned with defending their own positions and empires. So there may be a need at some time to break down the decentralised/ centralised structure and move back to either a centralised one or to a completely decentralised one. The change may be sufficient to re-energise those engaged in the procurement work and the processes which they use.

Effects of structure on corporate procurement policy, strategy and procedures

How do the various structures impinge on the corporate procurement policy, strategy and procedures?

It is not possible to be overly prescriptive about where the responsibilities for procurement strategy should lie as it will depend on the precise character of the structure. The following guidance needs to be taken as a starting point for development rather than as a set of rules.

1. Responsibility for development and application of corporate procurement policy and strategy

This obviously should rest at the centre in both the centralised and the centralised/decentralised structures. It is rather more complicated when it is a decentralised structure. In a group of business units, it depends on whether there is a corporate policy and a corporate strategy for all the units in the group or whether each unit has its own policy and strategy, as is usually the case in a conglomerate. Sometimes, there is a mix of corporate policy and strategy and individual business unit policy and strategy. In this situation, a corporate procurement policy and strategy will probably have to be developed for each business unit by its overall management.

2. Responsibility for corporate procurement procedures

It is easier to assign the responsibility for the development and implementation of procedures to units which are centralised and this is obviously very true when the procurement is centralised at the group centre. When the procurement is more decentralised by being dispersed throughout business units, the overall management of the business unit must be assigned the responsibility. In a centralised/decentralised structure, the centre may have responsibility for policy and strategy but it will be difficult for it to implement procedures when procurement is undertaken at the business unit level or below. Again, this means that the responsibility for implementation needs to be assigned to the overall management of the business unit.

3. Auditing procedures

Implementation is not the only thing which is affected by the structure. Auditing of compliance with procedures is also affected.

In a centralised structure, the responsibility for an audit to check compliance with procedures should not rest with the manager in charge of the procurement unit. There is an obvious conflict of interest. Usually, this is not a problem for organisations which have

---

an audit department; however, it can be for organisations which do not. Some other manager should be made responsible for the audit.

In a centralised/decentralised structure, the responsibility may rest with the centre as the centre's involvement with 'hands-on' management of contracts is likely to be less.

In a completely decentralised unit, the responsibility has to rest with the overall management of that unit.

CHAPTER 3

The content of a corporate procurement policy

Whatever appears in a procurement policy should be endorsed by senior management at the board level (or equivalent) of the organisation for use throughout the organisation. If this happens, the subject matter of the procurement policy will be the organisation's and not just the procurement department's.

Policies may vary from organisation to organisation, so here we give the main headings followed by guidance about what the corporate procurement policy should contain and why it should contain it. A template for a corporate procurement policy is available from the website *www.knowledgeaware.co.uk* and, subject to conditions listed on the website, it may be downloaded free of charge. The template may be modified to meet the exact needs of the organisation concerned.

The headings which a corporate procurement policy should address are:

- Definitions

- Applicability

- Compatibility with corporate policy, objectives and strategy

- Linking procurement strategy and procurement policy

- Structure of procurement and the roles of those engaged in it

- High-quality, innovative procurement

- Value

- Long-term view

- Procurement audits, performance measurement and continuous improvement

- Spend mapping, transaction cost management and risk management

- Relationship with stakeholders

- Compliance with central contracts

- Use of written contracts

- Use of competition

- Procurement ethics

- Fair trade

- Protecting the good name of the organisation

- Blame

- Fraud avoidance

- Legal compliance

- Training

- Fair treatment of suppliers, partnering and anti-discrimination approach

- Late payment of invoices

- Transparency, accountability and audit

- Confidentiality and commercial/intellectual property rights

- Consortia

- Annual report

- Environmental purchasing

- Health and safety

The remainder of the chapter covers these headings in more detail.

Definitions

The first step in any policy document is to define the subject matter of the policy. Procurement, purchasing, purchasing and contracts, purchasing and supply, purchasing and supply chain, supply chain, etc. are all overlapping terms which are sometimes used to mean the same thing and sometimes used to mean different things. The exact meaning can often only be judged by the context. It makes sense for the policy to make clear what it means when it says procurement (or whichever of the other expressions is being used).

In organisations where there are internal supply arrangements it can be helpful to have a definition of what constitutes external procurement (the supply of goods, services and works from outside the organisation) and what constitutes internal procurement (the supply of goods, services and works by another part of the organisation). It might be desirable to apply the same rules to internal procurement as to external procurement as this tests the competitive nature of any internal procurement, although there are sometimes human resource implications to doing this.

Applicability

Having defined what procurement is, it is now helpful to define its applicability. In some organisations, there are still various activities which are not considered to be procurement nor the responsibility of any professional procurement department. Examples are outsourcing, the procurement of advertising and other marketing services, temporary personnel services, legal services and so on. Ideally, the remit of professional procurement should be defined to cover all procurement in the organisation.

The applicability statement also needs to deal with the extent of the corporate procurement policy. Some organisations have subsidiaries. Some organisations are truly global and there are many more which are not global but which do have subsidiaries abroad. Is the corporate procurement policy to apply to all subsidiaries and be international in the sense that it applies to overseas operations?

> It is important to decide whether the corporate procurement policy applies to all parts of the organisation, including all subsidiaries at home and abroad.

The possibility of other legal systems and cultures affecting the policy and possibly rendering it inoperable also needs to be considered. Naturally, the scope of such considerations depends on the extent of the policy. In organisations with business interests abroad, it is necessary at each stage of the drafting of a corporate procurement policy to ask oneself whether there are any international implications which impinge on what is being drafted. This question should also be asked when drafting the corporate procurement strategy and the procedures.

Compatibility with corporate policy, objectives and strategy

The corporate procurement policy needs to make it clear that the objective of procurement is to support corporate policy objectives and strategies through the pursuit of value and not just 'savings'.

It is helpful to state briefly what the corporate policy objectives and strategy are. This may simply be a repetition of what appears in corporate policy/strategy documents or it might be a summary. Any need for confidentiality with respect to corporate policy and strategy can be an issue. There is not much point in referring to corporate policy objectives and strategy if they are considered to be confidential and known only to a very restricted circle of people. On the other hand, a user of the corporate procurement policy needs to understand what the contribution of procurement is to corporate policy objectives and strategy. Some balance has to be found.

Linking procurement strategy and procurement policy

This does not need to be any more than a statement which clarifies the role of procurement strategy in relation to procurement policy. Simply put, the strategy puts the policy into effect and the procedures spell out exactly how this is to be done.

The main reason for this statement is to help those less familiar with policies and strategies to understand how the two fit together. This can be helped by publishing the corporate procurement policy and the corporate procurement strategy as one document with each strategy set below the relevant policy. This device helps to establish a clear link.

Structure of procurement and the roles of those engaged in it

The procurement policy needs to make clear whether procurement is to be centralised, decentralised or managed using the centralised/decentralised approach. There is no need to go into detail about the exact structure as this should be covered in the corporate procurement strategy.

Any organisational structure for procurement has to take account of the structure of the organisation as a whole. If all the other departments of the organisation are decentralised, then it is unlikely that procurement will flourish if it alone has a strongly centralised structure. Presumably, the structure of the organisation has been selected in order to deliver the corporate policy objectives and the corporate strategy. As procurement is a part of this joint effort, the structure of any procurement activity will need to be compatible with the structure of the rest of the organisation.

For centralised or centralised/decentralised structures, this section of the policy should define the role of the central unit and its relationship with internal customers. For example, in a centralised structure, the head of procurement should be defined as being responsible for all (or most) procurement as well as procurement-related activities such as training, market research, procedures, systems, etc. In the centralised/decentralised structure, the head of procurement might be defined as responsible for some procurement and for many (possibly all) procurement-related activities. For decentralised procurement structures, this part of the policy may have to assign a responsibility to somebody in each business unit. For all structures, it helps to make it clear that any delegation must be to suitable staff (not to just any staff) and that a list of such staff must be maintained.

Detail should be given in the corporate procurement strategy. The policy's role is to establish as a high-level policy just how procurement in the organisation is to be structured.

```
State:

    •    whether centralised, decentralised or
         centralised/decentralised.

Also state if applicable:

    •    the role of the head of procurement;

    •    the responsibilities of any central unit;

    •    who is responsible in each business unit.
```

High-quality, innovative procurement

The corporate procurement policy should commit the organisation to high-quality, innovative procurement. High quality in this context means that the organisation will conduct its procurement in an ethical, fair and reasonable way while trying to take full advantage of its commercial position in the marketplace. Innovative means that the organisation is prepared to try new methods of procurement provided these do not conflict with the ideal of high quality.

Value

The prime objective of this policy is to establish value as the core objective of procurement. The policy should *stipulate* value as the objective of procurement in support of the organisation's overall policy and objectives. What value is in any particular case will depend on what is being procured. The policy needs to make this clear but it also needs to identify the various important attributes of value such as quality, delivery, user or internal customer satisfaction and whole-life cost.

The policy should state that this does not mean that price or cost cannot be the paramount concern. Most private and public sector organisations are likely to encounter such circumstances. An example is when the organisation is in serious financial trouble and procurement has a big role to play as a major cost-cutter.

Long-term view

This section introduces the long-term view as the time-span over which procurement should be judged.

Much procurement activity is limited by an obsession with short-term gains. This usually hampers the search for value. By adopting a long-term time-span and linking this with the search for value in support of the organisation's strategy, the policy both emphasises value as the key contribution of procurement and establishes an adequate time-span to ensure its achievement. This moves procurement away from short-termism.

Procurement audits, performance measurement and continuous improvement

This policy requires that procurement is regularly audited. It should establish continuous improvement as the fundamental reason for the audit. The audit should be more than just policing compliance with procedures. This does not mean that the audit will not be checking for compliance. Such checks are important because compliance should be a safeguard against fraud (which is discussed later in the policy). However, a major thrust of the audit should be to learn lessons and find better ways of doing things. This ethos and the attitude of the auditors are important drivers in the search for continuous improvement.

Measurement of procurement performance is an important matter which should be required by the corporate procurement policy. Procurement measurement is not always done even in the most professional of procurement departments. This is partly because it is not easy to do (although it is not impossible) and partly because there is often nobody particularly interested in the results outside of the procurement department. It is, however, very difficult to see how a procurement department can continuously improve if it is not measuring its performance. Measurement can also highlight the need for a change in approach.

The policy should sanction benchmarking as a possible means of identifying any need for change and improvement.

Spend mapping, transaction cost management and risk management

Spend mapping – consisting of expenditure discovery (finding out how much is spent, by whom, on what, with which suppliers and with what frequency) and expenditure consolidation (identifying market-facing categories of spend) – is essential to understanding and managing procurement. It is time-consuming and difficult to do because the information is almost never in a format which facilitates easy mapping and complete and/or reliable information is often not available. However, making spend mapping a requirement of the corporate procurement policy means that the mapping process receives the endorsement of the organisation once the policy has been endorsed by the its board-level management. This high-level approval might help overcome or, at least, reduce obstacles to spend mapping, such as opposition or indifference from some members of staff.

Transaction cost analysis is often neglected when assessing procurement but it should be required by the policy as large sums can be unnecessarily spent in transacting low-value procurement by using inefficient procurement processes.

Risk also needs to be systematically identified and managed. Risk is one of those aspects of procurement to which references are often made but there is usually not a lot of thought given to how it may be assessed and managed even though most procurement processes are intended to reduce risk. Risk is not easy to measure but selection of the most appropriate procurement process should take into account the need to manage risk.

Relationship with stakeholders

This part of the policy should require the involvement of stakeholders in procurement decisions. Stakeholders are those persons in the organisation who might be affected by a procurement decision. Internal customers are a special kind of stakeholder. Internal customers are those who will use the goods or services which have been bought. Internal customers may also be those persons who influence the procurement decision; for example, the IT department might be involved with the operations department in deciding what is the most appropriate IT system for operations. Both the IT department and the operations department are internal customers.

The finance department could be affected by the procurement decision. Finance is not an internal customer with respect to the operations IT system but it is a stakeholder.

Compliance with central contracts

There is little point in having central contracts and agreements if staff are allowed to disregard them. It should be a part of the policy that staff must use them wherever possible and reasons for any failure to comply should be recorded and reviewed, and might be subject to sanctions.

Use of written contracts

It might not always be appreciated that contracts do not need to be in writing and that a verbal agreement can be a binding legal contract. This policy should make it clear that verbal orders and contracts are to be avoided. This is an important stipulation in organisations where procurement is entirely decentralised.

Use of competition

The policy should stress the importance of competition. Competition should be made the organisation's preferred approach to its procurement. This should be obvious to procurement professionals but it may be less obvious to personnel who are not procurement professionals but who, nevertheless, have a procurement responsibility in a decentralised or centralised/decentralised environment.

Procurement ethics

All organisations should have a code of procurement ethics. This part of the policy stresses the need for the staff engaged in procurement to comply with it.

Fair trade

This policy rejects any procurement which might lead to unfair, unhealthy or unsafe exploitation of children, women and ethnic or religious groups.

Protecting the good name of the organisation

It should be a policy requirement that all procurement is conducted in such a way as to protect the good name of the organisation so as to avoid public relations embarrassment. This policy supports those dealing with procurement ethics and fair trade.

Blame

As has been previously stated in the policy, the organisation should welcome innovative approaches to procurement provided they do not infringe other aspects of the policy. The intention of the policy statement about blame is to encourage the pursuit of such innovation and to assure staff that they will not be blamed for errors provided they do not arise from negligence or disregard of procedures and instructions from management.

Fraud avoidance

Fraud avoidance can be assisted by having sound procedures and insisting that staff comply with them. The procedures need to require that there are adequate audit trails.

Fraud avoidance is not just in the interest of the organisation. Good fraud avoidance helps to protect the individual from incorrect suspicion of fraud because it makes successful fraud less likely (although, unfortunately, not impossible).

The policy statement should state the organisation's intention to combat fraud in procurement by means of procedures and audit trails and it should also assure staff of support if they draw to the organisation's attention possible incidences of fraud provided that the individual genuinely believes that there has been such an incident.

Legal compliance

This is a rather obvious policy statement that staff must comply with all aspects and intentions of the law when undertaking procurement work.

Training

This policy statement commits the organisation to procurement training. A large number of organisations undertake little or no procurement training. It is estimated that there are 200,000 plus persons undertaking procurement work in the United Kingdom of which probably less than a quarter have had any form of training. These figures have to be treated with caution but they show the reason for a commitment by the organisation to training in procurement.

Fair treatment of suppliers, partnering and anti-discrimination approach

The twofold purpose of a policy statement about fair treatment of suppliers is to assure them that they will be fairly treated and to emphasise this policy to employees. Employees can forget the need for fair treatment when trying to extract the last ounce of advantage for the procurement organisation. It is rarely in the interest of a procurement organisation to work in this way, especially in the long term. Economic circumstances do change and it is always possible that the supplier may at some time be able to turn the tables if it becomes the dominant partner in a commercial relationship.

Partnering might be an appropriate supplier relationship strategy and the policy should make it an option to be sought, but only when it is practicable and advantageous to do so.

The policy should also emphasise that there should be no discrimination against suppliers on the grounds of race, gender, etc.

Late payment of invoices

In some countries, legislation now requires invoices to be paid on time. However, even where this is not the case, late payment can be a cause of poor supplier relations. It is prudent for the organisation to make prompt payment a part of its corporate procurement policy.

Transparency, accountability and audit

This part of the policy simply requires that all procurement procedures and processes are transparent, accountable and auditable. This is an excellent place to emphasise again that staff are required to create audit trails.

Confidentiality and commercial/intellectual property rights

It should be part of any organisation's policy to safeguard its intellectual and commercial property rights and to require confidentiality from its suppliers in their dealings with it. The organisation should offer the same to the supplier organisations.

Consortia

This policy statement permits procurement to be undertaken as part of a consortium if this is likely to yield extra value. Consortia exist quite extensively in some parts of the public sector and, to some extent, in the private sector.

Annual report

This policy statement commits the organisation to the production of an annual report about its procurement. The report is an internal management report only, although it could be published more widely if this is required. The objective is to make it clear to all what procurement has achieved and what value it has generated. It is more difficult to produce a report in a decentralised structure than in any other and it is less clear to whom the report should be submitted so organisations with this type of structure will need to address this in the policy.

Environmental purchasing

This policy statement should commit the organisation to a green purchasing agenda. The precise agenda can be defined in another document. Many organisations now have a statement of how they will try to make their procurement environmentally friendly. This statement is often in addition to the normal procurement procedures to be discussed later in this book.

Health and safety

Similarly, there should be a policy statement committing the organisation to procurement which is compatible with the health and safety of all persons engaged in the procurement and supply, including those in all suppliers in the supply chain.

CHAPTER 4

The content of a corporate procurement strategy

While there should be a strategy for each policy, it is not always practical for there to be a procedure for each strategy. The strategies need to be embedded in the procedures in the sense that the actions required by the procedures will deliver the strategy and so meet the policy. Consequently, a single strategy may appear in many places in the procedures.

As there should be a strategy for each policy, we use the same headings as the previous chapter. Readers might wish to cross refer to the headings in that chapter.

Definitions

The *policy* defined procurement in terms of external and internal procurement.

The *strategy* can be used to make further definitive statements which amplify what the organisation's procurement is. For example, it can be used to give information about the total amount normally spent by the organisation in any 12-month period. This helps to fix the importance of procurement to the organisation, particularly if it is related to the organisation's total expenditure and its turnover or sales.

It can also be useful to define what is meant by supplies, services and works and to explain that the latter two are bought using contracts whereas supplies are normally purchased using orders (which, of course, legally are contracts but are usually not as detailed or as voluminous as contracts for services or works) and using framework agreements (which may or may not be contracts).

A useful addition is a statement about the organisation's belief in well conducted procurement and what value the organisation considers this will bring to its business. This helps establish procurement as an important, value-adding activity in the organisation.

Applicability

The aspects of applicability which should be covered in the policy are:

- the extent to which procurement policy is to apply, for example does it apply to outsourcing?

- the organisational and geographical applicability and the extent of such applicability taking into account the effect of other cultures and other legal systems.

The strategy needs to re-emphasise and amplify this policy requirement and explain any limitations which might apply to it.

Compatibility with corporate policy, objectives and strategy

The corporate procurement policy was linked to the corporate policy, corporate objectives and corporate strategy by setting value as the objective of procurement.

The strategy should discuss value in more detail and indicate those components which are crucial to the delivery of corporate aims and objectives.

Linking procurement strategy and procurement policy

The corporate procurement policy should have made it clear that the procurement strategy puts it into effect.

The corporate procurement strategy needs to make it clear that the strategies contained in the strategy document underpin the corporate procurement policy and have been selected to ensure that procurement delivers its contribution to the corporate policy, objectives and strategy.

Neither policy nor strategy (whether at the corporate or procurement levels) are fixed for all time. They will change depending on the challenges facing the organisation. The possibility of future change should be mentioned. The organisation should affirm its commitment to continuous improvement of its procurement and to innovation.

Depending on the structure, the organisation should assign the responsibility for making such changes. In the centralised and centralised/decentralised models this would be the person at the centre who is responsible for procurement. In decentralised models, the assignment of this responsibility would have to be to some person in each business unit. It should be somebody with authority, a senior person in the business unit.

Structure of procurement and the roles of those engaged in it

The corporate procurement policy will have made it clear whether the structure of procurement is to be decentralised, centralised or centralised/decentralised and where responsibility for procurement lies. The strategy now takes this and amplifies it.

A centralised structure and a centralised/decentralised structure will have an individual who will be the head of procurement (even if this is not the actual title) – see Table 4.1. The strategy should define the actual responsibilities of this individual. These include those which will be carried out on his or her behalf by the procurement staff. The responsibility of the head of procurement defines the role of the procurement department.

Possible responsibilities for a centralised structure could include:

- undertaking all procurement of significance;

- providing guidance about procurement matters;

- developing procurement policy, strategy and procedures, as needed, to meet changes required by the organisation's business;

Table 4.1 Responsibility for procurement

Structure	Responsibility for procurement
Centralised	Head of procurement for all procurement activities
Centralised/decentralised	Head of procurement mostly
Decentralised	Somebody in each unit of the decentralised structure

- responsibility for procurement training;

- managing best-practice procurement processes;

- reviewing proposals to place contracts for major procurements before these are submitted for approval;

- implementation of improved processes, e.g. e-procurement and purchase cards;

- compliance with legal requirements;

- performance measures;

- benchmarking;

- managing procurement contracts as appropriate and depending on whether the structure is centralised or centralised/ decentralised;

- outsourcing;

- spend and process mapping;

- transaction cost measurement and management;

- planning.

The full range of activities will depend on the organisation and its structure for procurement.

The objective is to make it clear what the responsibilities of the central procurement department are. In the centralised/decentralised model, it might be necessary to explain what the responsibilities are of the decentralised part of the procurement structure. The boundary between the central procurement department and the decentralised procurement structure should be delineated in the strategy.

In the decentralised structure, the responsibilities for procurement are devolved to the business units or below. This means that each business unit must adopt the roles set out above for a head of procurement in a centralised structure. If they do not, then procurement is not being managed, it is simply been done and the chances of it adding any value to the organisation are slim.

High-quality, innovative procurement

The corporate procurement policy commits the organisation to high-quality, innovative procurement.

The corporate procurement strategy should explain how this might be done. This might include benchmarking, networking with other organisations, document reviews (such as magazines, books and university research reports) and encouraging suggestions from members of staff.

This responsibility may be assigned to the central procurement function in a centralised or centralised/decentralised structure. It has to be assigned to each business unit in a decentralised structure. There is, however, always a doubt whether high-quality, innovative procurement will be achieved in a decentralised structure unless each unit in the decentralised organisation has its own procurement champion.

Value

The corporate procurement policy has established value as the core objective of procurement for the organisation. The strategy should describe how value is to be achieved.

The first step should be a review of whether any procurement is really needed. It is surprising how often goods and services are bought because an individual would like to have them rather than because the organisation really needs to buy them. The procedures will deal in detail with how this review should be done. The strategy needs to make it clear that it should be done and to state who should do it (usually this should be the person requiring the procurement answering to his or her management). The strategy should also say when it should be done (usually when the need is first identified) and make it clear that it is a management responsibility to ensure that such reviews are done thoroughly.

The strategy should now define value. Value is a difficult concept. Often, it is subjective. The word is frequently used without understanding. Value is, like beauty, very much in the eye of the beholder.

Value may be defined as the relationship between whole-life cost and the function and quality of what is being bought plus various other often indefinable attributes such as the satisfaction and perception associated with it.

- *Function* is the capacity of whatever is bought (whether goods, services or works) to do what is required of them. This should be defined in the specification.

- *Quality* is about the absence of failure over the reasonable lifetime of whatever has been procured.

- *Satisfaction* is the degree to which the users of the supplies, services or works feel that their needs have been met.

- *Perception* is the opinion of the users of the supplies, services or works that procurement has fulfilled its obligation by supplying them.

- *Other factors* which might be relevant to any consideration of value could include environmental considerations and health and safety factors.

- *Whole-life cost* is the total of price, transaction costs, delivery costs, installation costs, storage costs, maintenance costs, consumption costs and disposal costs, as well as costs such as insurance and taxation, if applicable.

The procedures should discuss how the concept of value should be applied. The purpose of the strategy is to introduce it as a mandatory concept.

The strategy should acknowledge that there are a lot of occasions when value is really nothing more than price. Obvious examples are common items, like stationery, personal computers and other desktop equipment, which have become almost like commodities.

Long-term view

The strategy should give support to the policy requirement that a long-term view be taken. This could be achieved by providing examples of ways in which procurement can develop value over the longer term, e.g. by means of soundly constructed contracts, good contract management, improved procurement processes, and enhanced capability and flexibility. The strategy should acknowledge that other approaches are possible and will be used subject to their conforming with the procurement policy and legal requirements.

Procurement audits, performance measurement and continuous improvement

The strategy should require that all procurement work, including any delegated dispersed work, be subject to audit as required. The audits should be conducted by neutral persons and the results published to interested parties, including those engaged in procurement. A response to the audit will be required from the appropriate management. Recommendations must be implemented. It helps if the senior management of the organisation monitor that implementation has taken place.

Regarding performance measurement, the strategy should say who should develop the measures and benchmarks and who should apply them. Again there should be a report made to the organisation's senior management.

The appropriate person to be responsible for the implementation of recommendations and for performance measurement is the head of procurement in the centralised structure. In the decentralised model, it is the appropriate management of each separate business unit. In the centralised/decentralised model, the head of procurement will have to work with the management of the units to which procurement has been delegated in order to ensure that measures and benchmarks are agreed and implemented. The strategy will need to make this clear.

Spend mapping, transaction cost management and risk management

The policy has established the need for spend mapping, transaction cost analysis and risk measurement. The strategy assigns responsibility for these tasks and sets a time-frame during which they should be conducted. Conducted here means either undertaking them from scratch or reviewing previous work to see if the conclusions drawn from it are still valid.

Spend mapping should not be a one-off exercise. Changes in the organisation's business and the markets in which it operates will be reflected in the spend pattern. This in turn affects procurement. The same can be said of transaction cost management and risk.

The uses of the spend maps – basically the consolidation of requirements for the purposes of economies of scale – should be described. The strategy should also state that future IT system upgrades (usually in the finance department) must take account of the need for spend mapping.

Spend information should be plotted on the four-box risk–spend matrix commonly used to identify possible contract strategies. (This will be discussed in more detail in later parts of this book.)

Assessment of risk is not easy and the strategy should either describe how this should be done or it should assign a responsibility for finding the most appropriate method depending on circumstances.

Relationship with stakeholders

To support the policy of involvement of stakeholders in procurement decision-making and to develop teamworking, the strategy should require those engaged in procurement to identify stakeholders and involve them as appropriate in the various stages of the procurement.

The strategy should recognise that involvement may not be necessary or practical in some procurement. This is true of frequently purchased goods or services where the specification is long established and recognised as sufficient by all parties and the supply markets for these goods and services are stable.

The strategy should also recognise that there can be many stakeholders who can be a very varied and far-flung group of people. It might therefore be only practical for consultation to take place with a representative sample. The selection of those persons for consultative purposes should be left to the discretion of those doing the procurement.

The strategy should make the role of the stakeholders clear. Their role is to assist those engaged in doing the procurement to achieve a sound outcome for each and every procurement.

Compliance with central contracts

Maverick spending is the independent purchasing of non-standard goods and services when standard ones are available under the cover of centrally agreed contracts. The arguments against it are as follows:

- It diminishes the possible benefits of economies of scale.

- It often means the introduction of goods or services which are not to the agreed specification and therefore involve extra cost in maintaining or otherwise supporting them.

- The person doing the maverick purchasing is spending their time doing that when it is not their function or expertise.

The strategy should impose on management of each department or function the duty to ensure that its staff complies with the central contracts.

Use of written contracts

The policy should require that contracts should be in writing whenever possible for the obvious reason of recording what has been agreed. Written contracts can help avoid disputes although they certainly do not eliminate them. Written contracts also provide part of the audit trail and they can be a safeguard against fraud although they are not foolproof in this respect.

The strategy should require the management of all departments involved in procurement to ensure that contracts are put into writing whenever possible.

Use of competition

The strategy should require those engaged in procurement to take appropriate steps to ensure the use of competition wherever possible. This requires cooperation between those parties involved in the procurement so that the procurement is designed to stimulate competition. This might, for example, mean avoiding single sourcing. It could also mean splitting the procurement requirement into packages which are attractive to the suppliers so that the packages encourage competition, possibly by interesting new sources of supply.

The strategy should put a time limit on the duration of contracts as competition atrophies when the contracts are very long. On the other hand, very short durations impose a burden on both those doing the procurement and on the suppliers and contractors who have to compete for the work. Those engaged in procurement should always be mindful of the costs to suppliers of preparing bids.

Procurement ethics

Every organisation should have a code of procurement ethics. The strategy should emphasise the corporate procurement policy's requirement that staff comply with this code.

Fair trade

The strategy should require the development of specific approaches to guard against the exploitation of disadvantaged groups, encourage equal opportunities and protect the environment.

The strategy could also require pre-qualified suppliers and their suppliers to have their own fair trade policies which should be similar in principle to those of the procurement organisation.

If there are suppliers with no fair trade strategy, then it might be necessary to encourage suppliers to develop them. The strategy should also address what will happen to suppliers who claim to meet these strategies but subsequently fail to do so in practice.

Protecting the good name of the organisation

The strategy should explain why protecting the good name of the organisation is important. It should require management to take action both to ensure that the staff are mindful of this need in their dealings with suppliers and to help staff who may be failing to comply with this requirement.

Blame

The strategy should state what management is expected to do when staff make mistakes. This is not to apportion blame but to draw the attention of the staff to the mistake and give guidance about how to avoid making it in the future. Staff who fail to respond might need to be subject to the disciplinary procedures of the organisation and the strategy should make this clear.

Fraud avoidance

The strategy should require sound, up-to-date procurement procedures and impose, on a nominated person, the responsibility for ensuring that they are kept up to date. In a centralised/decentralised structure, this may be the head of procurement. In an organisation whose procurement structure is decentralised, it will be necessary to nominate a manager in each of the decentralised units.

An assurance should be given to whistleblowers to the effect that they will be protected provided their whistleblowing is based on genuine reasons even if they turn out to be wrong. Whistleblowing requires courage but, if done for mistaken reasons, can cause an enormous amount of distress. The procurement organisation needs to face up to this and be prepared to take steps to cope with any difficulties which may arise even though the eventuality is likely to be a rarity.

As previously mentioned, the strategy should require clear audit trails and nominate the bodies responsible for auditing. Audits should be frequently conducted.

Legal compliance

The procurement organisation should require its staff to comply with the law and it should be prepared to offer training to ensure that they do so. The responsibility for selecting and authorising training should be stated. This responsibility will again depend on the structure of procurement in the organisation.

The strategy should also address the need for audits to ensure that legal requirements have been met and deal with what is to be done if there has been any failure to comply with them.

Training

The strategy should assign responsibility for developing or employing a way of assessing training needs. It should require staff to participate in tests to discover any gaps which can be rectified by appropriate training. The strategy should also assign the responsibility for arranging and/or developing training and, of course, staff should be made available to attend any training.

The structure of procurement in the organisation will again determine who is responsible for these actions.

Fair treatment of suppliers, partnering and anti-discrimination approach

Those engaged in procurement should always be mindful of the costs to suppliers of preparing bids. Transaction costs are an unavoidable part of all procurement processes. If suppliers are to remain solvent, they will have to recoup these costs somewhere and this can only be done when they are successful in winning contracts. Although this might seem of little importance to procurement specialists, it should be part of their role not to exacerbate the costs of suppliers. Thus the strategy should require those engaged in procurement to minimise suppliers' transaction costs wherever possible.

The strategy should also require that racial, religious, gender, physical disability considerations or the sexuality of persons involved in business relationships are not permitted to impede such relationships (see Figure 4.1). Guidance should be given about how this might be avoided.

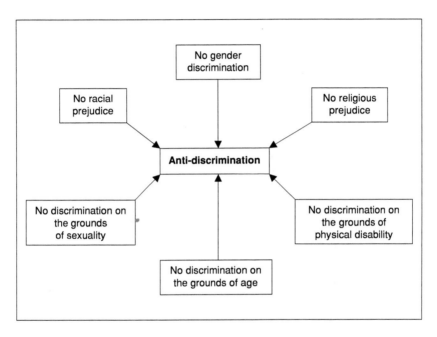

Figure 4.1 Considerations for an anti-discrimination strategy.

The procurement organisation may wish to support partnering as a preferred mode of working with suppliers in appropriate circumstances, in which case it should state what those circumstances are or require that they are compiled and published.

Although it might be infrequently used, there should be a supplier complaint procedure in place to enable suppliers to make justified complaints against unfair procurement practice. Most procurement specialists are either unaware of the need for such a procedure or would not favour the organisation having one. However, if the organisation is committed to treating suppliers fairly, it should ensure that they have a recognised means of making heard any complaint about unfair treatment. The strategy should require such a procedure.

Suppliers' Complaints Procedure

Enables suppliers to make justified complaints against unfair practices

The organisation should impose on itself the requirement not to use suppliers which abuse disadvantaged groups, discriminate on the grounds of gender, race, disability, etc. and do not take care of the environment.

Procurement organisations should consider whether they wish to use local suppliers preferentially. This is normally not recommended as a blanket policy. However, it may be sound in certain circumstances. The strategy should address this issue.

Late payment of invoices

The strategy should require all members of staff to take steps to ensure that invoices are paid on time.

In many countries, there are still many incidences when invoices are not paid on time and many organisations, particularly smaller ones, are obliged to wait for considerable periods of time for payment. Apart from the ethical considerations, widespread on-time payment could avoid the possibility of legislation which will compel punctual payment. Such legislation will inevitably impose an extra administrative burden on procurement organisations and it might be more prudent to adopt a strategy to pay on time.

Transparency, accountability and audit

The strategy should assign the responsibility for ensuring that this aspect of the policy is implemented and require all members of staff to comply with it.

Confidentiality and commercial/intellectual property rights

Commercial and intellectual property rights have revenue implications for an organisation whether through their exploitation or through their neglect. The strategy should require that these considerations are taken into account in any contract which might be let by the procurement organisation. While they are often not uppermost in the minds of those responsible for letting contracts, a duty to take such rights into account should be imposed on them.

Commercial and intellectual property rights	=	$, £, euros, yen, rupiah, rials, etc.

The strategy should require the use of confidentiality agreements to maintain appropriate levels of secrecy with respect to the procurement organisation's affairs and with respect to the affairs of its suppliers.

The strategy should also require compliance with any legal requirements regarding disclosure of information.

Consortia

The strategy should define the circumstances when the use of consortia is permitted, for example when there are possibilities of transaction cost savings, value maximisation from demand consolidation, etc. The strategy should also draw the attention of those who might be engaged in establishing and operating consortia of possible competition law implications.

Annual report

The responsibility for producing an annual procurement report should be assigned to an appropriate officer depending on the structure of procurement in the organisation. The strategy should state what should go in the report, for example improvement targets, dates for meeting them, etc. The report should discuss progress in meeting such targets and it should also set targets for the new year. In this way, the report becomes the basis for a procurement plan for the next 12 months.

Environmental purchasing

The strategy should define the procurement organisation's approach to environmental purchasing. As a minimum this should:

- impose on managers in all departments the responsibility to consider the environmental effects of their requirements before authorising procurement;

- require that appropriate records are kept to demonstrate that this has been done;

- require that specifications take account of the environment;

- favour the adoption of the least environmentally damaging option – both staff and suppliers should be made aware of the organisation's approach to environmental issues;

- require the development of a guide to environmental procurement – in this case, it should impose the duty to produce such a guide on an appropriate officer;

- require that suppliers' green credentials are taken into consideration during pre-qualification.

Health and safety

As a minimum, the following could form the basis of a strategic approach to health and safety in procurement:

- health and safety issues to be taken into account when authorising any procurement;

- specifications to take account of the need for health and safety;

- subject to legal permissibility, health and safety criteria to be used as evaluation criteria when awarding orders or contracts;

- awareness of health and safety issues to be a part of the procurement training of staff;

- suppliers to be made aware of the procurement organisation's own health and safety policy.

CHAPTER 5

Corporate procurement procedures – taking some decisions

One size does not fit all

Procedures need to support the corporate procurement policy and to embed the procurement strategy. Above all, they need to explain how things should be done.

In every organisation, procurement is an activity concerned with the management of money and the supply chain in the pursuit of corporate objectives. It is often assumed that whatever is applicable to organisations with large spends will be applicable to organisations with small spends. Similarly, it may be assumed that small spends can be treated in exactly the same way as large spends. The fallacy of these assumptions is very quickly realised by anybody drafting procurement procedures.

The purchasing or procurement cycle consists of the following steps:

- Identify the need and define the requirement.

- Obtain authorisation to proceed.

- Undertake a strategic procurement analysis and develop a contract strategy.

- Identify potential suppliers.

- Obtain offers.

- Evaluate and refine offers.

- Let the contract.

- Manage the contract and the supply.

- Close out the contract.

All of these steps need to be covered by the procedures but they do not need to be undertaken in exactly the same way for all procurement. Consider a procurement with an annual spend representing 10 per cent of an organisation's sales turnover or, in the public sector, 10 per cent of a departmental budget. The spend is of high risk, which means that the organisation, whether in the private or public sector, will suffer some considerable harm if the supply is in any way defective (for example, deliveries are late, the quality is inadequate, the product or service does not do what it is supposed to, etc.).

For a procurement of this nature, all of the above steps need to be carried out thoroughly and in detail. Careful identification of the need (saying exactly what we want to do) and defining the requirement (producing a specification of something which will meet the need) are obviously crucial steps which will ensure that we get a product or a service which will not fail either unexpectedly or unreasonably and that quality will be 'built in' right from the start.

Similarly, the strategic procurement analysis and the contract plan will be steps which require considerable thought and development to ensure that we identify the right sort of supplier relationship and develop the most appropriate contract to support that relationship. It is also crucial to identify suppliers with whom we can work and who will respond positively within the relationship.

Obtaining and processing the offers together with their evaluation and refinement must ensure that we get the best deal. This is particularly important to us considering the size of the spend and the degree of the risk involved. We need to let the contract professionally so that it is clear what the contract is and so that there are no loose ends such as inaccurate verbal representations on which one of the parties is placing reliance for some reason or another. Disappointment when the representation is revealed to be a chimera could have the most serious effects: it is always better to avoid this situation if at all possible.

Contract management and contract close out will also be important. With a procurement of this importance, we cannot leave things unmanaged in the hope that delivery will be on time, on specification, etc. We need to manage the supplier and to avoid or resolve problems when they arise. We also need to ensure when the contract is complete that the parties agree it is complete, that all claims and disputes have been resolved, that there are no expensive law suits lurking in the background and that warranties are in place and will be honoured.

Now consider a procurement which is low risk and low spend, perhaps only of petty cash significance. Low risk means that supply failure really will not affect things much one way or the other.

Of course, the need should still be identified and the requirement defined but this is likely to be straightforward. Both processes are likely to be done in very rapid succession and they might even run into one another. It is quite likely that a proprietary specification will be used.

The strategic procurement analysis and the development of a contract strategy are likely to be swift decisions to find and buy from one supplier who can deliver as required. Potential supplier identification is likely to be done at the desk either from a catalogue or by means of a few telephone calls. It is quite possible that a supplier has been used previously and the requirement will be single sourced with that supplier.

There is often little or no need to develop a contract specifically, although it is prudent to try and ensure that the purchase is done using the purchasing organisation's own terms and conditions. Letting the contract is usually not much more than sending an order and the management is likely to be no more than the odd telephone call or e-mail. Contract close-out will not be done.

In these two scenarios, the same sorts of things have been done but they have been done very differently.

Using the risk–spend matrix in decision-making

Procedures need to take account of this variability. There is no point at all in applying the same rules to the same degree to all procurements. The key to making any decision is the relationship between relative procurement spend and risk to the procurement organisation. This relationship is a well known, well defined one as shown in Figure 5.1. There are many versions of this model and the labels in the boxes are intended to show what the procurement organisation should be trying to do.

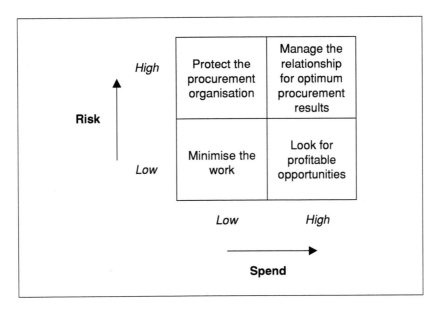

Figure 5.1 Risk–spend matrix.

Any procedures should be trying to support the objectives shown as labels in the boxes. However, to write procedures which do so, decisions about spend and risk need to be taken.

There are three important questions to ask about spend. Firstly, should there only be one boundary between low and high spend? Figure 5.1 suggests that there should and that it should apply to separate low-risk/low-spend procurement from low-risk/high-spend procurement and that the same boundary should separate high-risk/low-spend procurement from high-risk/high-spend procurement. However, it is important not to become spellbound by diagrams and models. They are tools to be used and adapted. They are not cast iron rules.

The second question is whether there should be an ultra-low category of spend, particularly for the low-risk/low-spend category. This is effectively dividing this box into two not necessarily equal areas. Whether this is needed depends on where the boundary between high and low spend has been set. Some organisations set this very low so that all low-spend/low-risk procurement is effectively ultra-low. Some organisations set this much higher.

For example, in organisations in the UK, this might be as high as £20,000 or more. If this is the case, then there is an argument for treating procurement worth, say, £500 or less as needing different processes to procurement between £500 and £20,000. Of course, £500 might be deemed to be far too low a threshold for ultra-low purchasing and it is not intended to suggest that this should be a threshold.

The third question is: what should be the spend amounts for each boundary or threshold? The answer to this question is that it depends on the organisation. Many public sector bodies tend to have lower thresholds than those used in the private sector but this is not an invariable rule. The decision has to be a part of the process of developing the procedures. Decisions about how to manage a procurement cycle for a procurement above or below a certain threshold help to fix what that threshold should be.

Just as there can be different thresholds for spend, so there can be different risk thresholds as well. Where the boundaries for risk between the different boxes in Figure 5.1 should be set depends on how risk averse an organisation is. There is no particularly good reason for *not* being risk averse unless great caution is spoiling advantageous opportunities at low or manageable moderate risk.

When the decisions about spend and risk have been made an organisation's spend–risk matrix might look something like Figure 5.2.

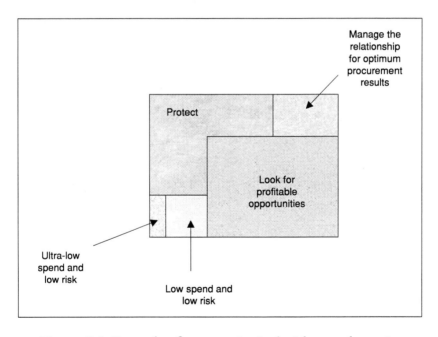

Figure 5.2 Example of an organisation's risk–spend matrix.

What sort of things should be covered in procedures?

A clue has already been given when the steps of the procurement cycle were mentioned above. The following should be covered or at least considered:

- identification of need;

- development of the requirement;

- drafting of specifications;

- authorisation to proceed with procurement;

- development of a strategic procurement approach if needed;

- development of an appropriate contract strategy;

- identification of suppliers using pre-qualification and/or qualification;

- development of the invitation to tender or the draft contract for negotiation;

- tendering and negotiation;

- letting of the contract;

- contract management;

- data management;

- contract close-out;

- low value;

- delegated procurement;

- procurement cards;

- e-procurement.

In Europe, utilities and the public sector will need to take account of the various EC Procurement Directives and the public sector will also need to take account of the GATT rules if necessary.

Many of the above are affected by the decisions regarding spend and risk.

Types of procurement

There are two types of procurement:

- those that require the compilation of a definition of a requirement, assessing markets, finding suppliers, developing a contract and the implementation of processes to let a contract;

- those that are essentially repeat purchases from a designated supplier sometimes under some form of framework agreement or call-off arrangement. (Note that the *original* letting of the framework agreement or call-off arrangement falls into the first category above.)

Procedures tend to be written around the first category and this book describes an approach to such procurements. For the procurements described in the second category, the following have all been carried out previously:

- the need;

- the requirement;

- the specification;

- the strategic approach;

- the contract strategy;

- the identification of suppliers;

- tendering and negotiation.

Such procurements might be linked to some form of stock control. It is then the stock control system which generates the order. Generally, such orders are raised, approved or authorised and sent out to the supplier. This constitutes the letting of a contract for repeat procurements. However, aspects such as contract management, data management and contract close-out still need to be undertaken.

The style of procedures

Procurement procedures are never likely to be favourite reading and so they should be short and reader friendly. However, this is easier to say than it is to do. The author recalls that in one organisation, an obsession with explaining the reason for everything led to an enormous set of procedures and a storm of protest about its length and readability. This meant that an abbreviated version had to be hastily produced but the damage had been done and the procedures had lost all credibility.

Procedures should written so as to make it clear what has to be done. Explanation of why something needs to be done is really a training responsibility but it is important that staff understand why otherwise they are likely to be doubtful of the value of what they are doing. This will make them sceptical about compliance.

Having a good layout with lots of white space, keeping sentences short, making it clear what is mandatory and what is discretional, keeping references to other parts of the procedures or other documents to a minimum and keeping the procedures themselves as simple as possible can all help readability and use by practitioners.

It is also important to bear in mind the reasons for having procedures when drafting them. These have been discussed in Chapter 1.

Mandatory and discretional requirements

A key objection to procedures is that they fit a straitjacket on people – and so they should, but not to the extent that they destroy all originality. It is therefore very important to say what words shall be used to designate a mandatory requirement with which compliance is totally required and what words shall designate discretion.

Words such as 'shall' and 'must' are mandatory words. They permit no deviation. Words such as 'may' or 'might' are permissive and leave things open to the reader of the procedures to use his or her discretion. This is no different to the words used for these purposes in contracts.

The difficulty lies in deciding what needs to be mandatory and what may be discretional. Erring too much on the mandatory side runs the risk of making things mandatory when the circumstances might require a more flexible approach. When drafting procedures, it is not always possible to know when flexibility will be needed. The best approach is for the writer to consult with procurement colleagues and stakeholders about this. For every proposed mandatory stipulation ask the question: 'In what circumstances could this not apply and flexibility be needed?'

Governance and management of procedures

Procedures need to be reviewed and changed from time to time and there needs to be somebody in the organisation who has the responsibility to initiate action to do this.

In a centralised or centralised/decentralised structure the most obvious person is the head of procurement. In a decentralised structure there needs to be somebody designated to undertake this in each of the decentralised units. From time to time, representatives of each unit will need to compare procedures and standardise them if they are not to become too widely divergent.

CHAPTER 6

The role of the internal customer

All procurement starts with the identification of the need. This is then developed into a requirement, usually by drafting a specification. Finally, thought has to be given to the commercial information which is required in order to obtain a quotation from the marketplace, whether this quotation results from negotiation or from a formal tendering approach or a combination of both.

The internal customer has a key role in the performance of these activities (see Figure 6.1). All of what follows is needed for major requirements. For less important requirements, some judgement will be needed as the same rigour will not be necessary and the procedures will have to reflect the need for this flexibility.

Identification of the need

It is the internal customer who recognises that there is some need to be satisfied. This is true whether the need is a new one or whether it is something which has been recognised in the past and for which there is an ongoing demand, i.e. a repeat procurement.

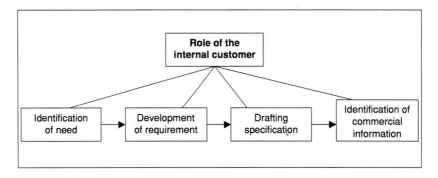

Figure 6.1 Role of the internal customer.

Developing the requirement is different to identifying the need. For example, while the need might be to put a picture on a wall, the requirement could be a hook but it could also be a nail or glue. It could also be a recess cut into the wall and no doubt there are other possibilities. If the need is more narrowly defined, for example if it were to *hang* a picture on a wall, then both glue and the possibility of a recess in the wall are ruled out, but it would still be possible to use a hook or a nail or anything else from which a picture could be hung. The important point is that by keeping the need very broad, there is usually a possibility of a much bigger range of requirements from which to choose.

Initially, the need should be identified in outline only. For a major project, it will be helpful to examine the justification for the project and then develop a statement of the need from this. The greater the complexity of likely requirement, the more time should be taken to identify the need. Similarly, the more complex the need, the more general it should be kept as this will help identify a greater number of possible requirements which will satisfy it.

Once the need has been identified in very general terms, some degree of specificity will be required to arrive at requirements which really will satisfy the need.

This adding of specificity is the first step in developing and selecting a requirement. But before going too far with developing the requirement, the need to avoid unnecessary expenditure and concerns for the environment demand that the need is examined to see whether it really is necessary. After all, the best way to avoid harming the environment is to consume less. The internal customer should ask: 'Is the need really needed?' and 'Could we manage without it?' If the answers are no and yes respectively, not only is the environment helped but the organisation's money is also saved.

An outline of the process is given in Figure 6.2.

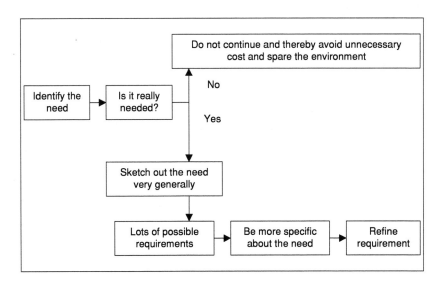

Figure 6.2 Identification of need and requirements.

The procedures should give the internal customer guidance about identifying the need. Firstly, the procedures should explain what a need is and why it is important. They should stress the importance of identifying the need and not jumping to the requirement. The procedures should require the use of the two questions 'Is the need really needed?' and 'Can we manage without it?' as part of the organisation's commitment to the environment.

The requirement

The next step is for the internal customer to examine all the acceptable requirements which might meet the need. This involves two separate steps. The first is to describe all the requirements and the second is to evaluate them and reject those which are unlikely to satisfy the need. The objective should be to ensure that there are several requirements which will meet the need. Having more than one potential requirement is helpful because:

- It facilitates the use of performance specifications instead of strict technical specifications which describe a specific product or service. This permits suppliers to use their expertise to offer options which the internal customer has not considered. These could be both commercially and technically advantageous.

- It could promote competition. Reducing the need to just one requirement can mean no competition if there is only one supplier which can supply the need. Although the purchasing organisation can use a number of ruses to try and conceal this from the supplier, it is quite possible that the supplier will be aware of the situation and will bid high accordingly.

- It permits a proper cost-benefit or value evaluation to be applied to the bids of possible suppliers.

Of course, there will be occasions when there is genuinely only one requirement which will do. If this can be supplied by a number of suppliers, then competition will still be possible. If it can genuinely only be supplied by one supplier, then a sole source situation really does exist.

Developing the specification – performance or technical?

Performance specifications describe what we want the requirement to do, they do not describe the requirement. A performance specification should contain details of maximum and minimum performance as well as typical performance. Such specifications are sometimes called output specifications as they are a description of the requirement's output.

On the other hand, a technical specification will describe the requirement in terms of its physical attributes (size, material, viscosity, density, crystal structure, strength, colour, texture, etc.) and possibly in terms of its chemical composition. A technical specification might define the manufacturing process for the requirement. A technical specification for a service will define what the service providers will do in sufficient detail for the service provider to do it. A performance specification will define the results required from the successful performance of the service.

The advantage of a performance specification is that it allows a supplier to suggest solutions to meet the requirement. This is particularly useful for services when a precise description of the service might be written by a purchasing organisation which does not have either the expert knowledge or the experience of the service. The likelihood is that important aspects will be omitted or that there will be a tendency to overspecify in an effort to 'get the requirement right'. The supplier, of course, does have both the knowledge and the expertise and should be in a better position to assess the precise nature of the service which is required. Performance requirements can also be useful when specifying equipment. For example, the performance of an office printer could be defined by stating the sort of printing which is required (e.g. black and white, colour diagrams or full colour printing), the size of runs, the speed which is required, ink consumption rates and so on.

What the procedures should say about specifications

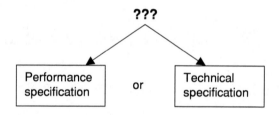

The procedures should require the internal customer to use performance specifications where possible and suitable. However, there are many occasions when these are not suitable. This is particularly true in manufacturing when the procurement organisation needs to specify a precise requirement to fit into its product. It is also true of repeat procurements. There are also occasions when it is easier to simply specify a branded good although the procedures should require the internal customer to add the words 'or similar' if there is no particular need to buy only the identified brand of goods.

The procedures should give the internal customer some guidance about drafting specifications. Figure 6.3 gives some examples of what *not* to include in a specification. For instance, the internal customer should ask whether each feature described in the specification is really needed. The specification should be kept short and readable but it needs to include everything which is required. Suppliers should not be expected to guess the requirements of the procurement organisation and it always needs to be remembered that it is these requirements which are the reason for the relationship between both the buyer and the seller. The specification of the requirements will become a crucial part of the contract between the two parties.

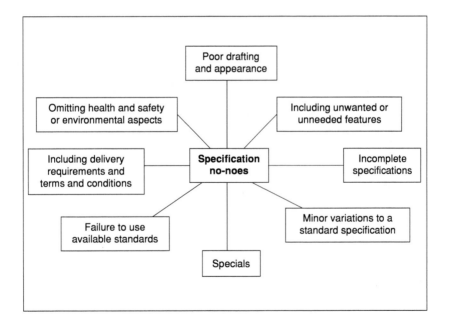

Figure 6.3 Specification no-noes.

The internal customer should guard against specifying 'specials' when a standard product will do. Customising costs money as it will usually require special action or treatment by the supplier. Recognised standards such as British Standards, the EN standards, etc. should be used wherever possible. Smaller procurements are likely to require less detail and the procedures need to make sure that the effort put into drafting the specification should be commensurate with the risk and the amount of the spend.

Key aspects which should be included are health and safety and the environment. They should be built into the specification so that the supplier is obliged to take them into account from the outset.

A specification should not contain delivery requirements or terms and conditions. It should deal with the description of the product or service which is required.

The procedures should make it clear that the internal customer should use existing specifications wherever possible, although it may be necessary to update this to take account of any changes such as legal requirements, technological changes or changes in the nature of the requirement itself. It is, however, important that the internal customer refrains from introducing minor variations into an existing specification which effectively make it into a new specification.

The procedures should require consultation with appropriate parties inside the organisation, such as finance, legal, procurement and quality departments, and, for complex requirements, consultation might also be required with external bodies such as other purchasers, universities, standards-making bodies and professional institutes.

An important stipulation which the procedures should make is to require the specification to be complete. Omissions are always costly, especially if the procurement organisation tries to change the specification after the contract has been let. If necessary the internal customer should establish a drafting panel to ensure that there are no omissions. This panel could include the departments mentioned above and it could also include representatives from the other bodies provided that they are willing.

For complex specifications, it is unlikely that a single internal customer will have the expertise and the knowledge to draft the specification and the procedures should require that the internal customer establish a drafting group with the necessary experts.

Involving the suppliers

Sometimes, the internal customer does not have the technical knowledge to sufficiently define the requirement. In these circumstances, internal customers might approach suppliers for information about their products.

There are several dangers if this is done in an ad hoc manner. Firstly, any supplier which sees the possibility of lucrative business will try to condition the internal customer. The conditioning, which might be so subtle that the internal customer is not conscious of it, will have three prime objectives (see Figure 6.4). The first objective will be to narrow down the requirement to what the supplier can supply. The supplier might try to discourage the investigation of other options from other suppliers. Secondly, the supplier will be trying to find out what the budget is for the procurement so that it will know at what level to price if asked to do so. The third objective is to build up a sense of obligation so that the internal customer and, hopefully, the organisation in general feels a debt of gratitude to the supplier for all the work which it has done in helping to define the requirement. In certain circumstances, this might lead to tenders being evaluated or negotiations conducted more favourably than they should be or, possibly, there being no competition at all.

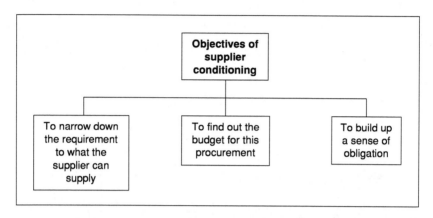

Figure 6.4 Objectives of supplier conditioning.

The procedures need to address this issue. The usual approach is for a request for information (RFI) to be issued to suitable suppliers. The procedures should clearly define the circumstances in which suppliers should be approached, who should be involved in making the approach, how it should be made and what the mechanism is for gaining approval before any approach is made. The approval mechanism is important as there is a risk of erosion of competition owing to skilful supplier conditioning. In centralised and centralised/decentralised organisations, approval should usually be given by the head of procurement acting in concert with the head of the department responsible for defining the requirement. In decentralised organisations, the procedures should specify who should issue an approval.

Having obtained approval, the next step is to identify the suppliers. (This matter is discussed in Chapter 9.) It might be necessary at this stage to consider the pre-qualification of the suppliers which have been identified. (Pre-qualification is discussed in a later chapter.) However, it might not be possible at this stage to undertake a full pre-qualification as it will not be certain whether the supplier can offer a requirement which is likely to be of interest. It might therefore be necessary to split the pre-qualification into two parts, the first to establish the potential supplier's suitability and willingness to make a proposal and the second to establish the supplier's ability to supply if the proposal is acceptable to the procurement organisation.

The procedures should require the approach to be made in writing and for suppliers to respond in writing. Any request for a proposal issued by the procurement organisation to suppliers should make it clear whether the procurement organisation is prepared to pay for any work done by the supplier in making a proposal. Usually, procurement organisations are reluctant to do this but it might be necessary if a desirable supplier does not see the procurement organisation as a customer worth cultivating; the supplier is then reluctant to invest the time in something which might not bring any reward. Again, the procedures need to address this issue.

The process of issuing a request for information and for receiving and evaluating the information should be similar to the process for inviting tenders.

The request for information should describe the need and leave the supplier to suggest possible solutions. The need should be described in such a way that the possible requirements are not skewed to some particular type of solution. This is very much the same as using a performance specification instead of a detailed technical specification or a brand name.

It is not unusual to ask the supplier to give estimated or ball-park figures of the likely cost of what they are proposing. The proposals need to be evaluated by the procurement organisation. This is best done by a panel of experts, each member of which evaluates all the proposals independently and scores them for their technical merit in meeting the need. At some point, these scorings are circulated with justifications for them to the other members of the panel, so that each member is in possession of each other member's scores and justifications. The panel should then meet to discuss the scores and justifications.

If there is unanimity, then the discussion will be short. If there is any disparity, the panel should explore why these exist and see how sound they are. The objective is to arrive at a number of solutions which could meet the need and therefore a list of suppliers which will be invited to tender or to negotiate.

It is unlikely that procedures will be able to specify how the scoring should be done as this will vary from product to product and from service to service. The procedures should require that scoring is used and that the scoring should be conducted independently followed by reconciliation along the lines described above.

Commercial information

The procedures should require the internal customer to identify the commercial information needed to buy the requirement. This information should include the following:

- *The normal quantity required at any one time.* For services, this will be the extent of the service, e.g. clean one floor or clean the whole building.

- *The frequency or repetitiveness of the demand.* This is how many times a year there will be a demand for the requirement and for how many years a demand is likely to continue.

- *The likely complexity of the procurement.* A construction project is much more complex than the purchase of stationery because of the timescales, the number of suppliers involved and the complexity of the requirement.

- *The likely unit whole-life cost of the requirement.* For simple items, this will probably be no more than the price.

- *The risk if there were a failure to obtain the supplies.*

- *When the delivery of the requirement is required.* This could mean when it starts and when it finishes. It applies to supplies, services and works.

It might be necessary for the internal customer to consult with colleagues in either procurement or in other departments to obtain this information. The information will mostly be best estimates but they must, of course, be as accurate as possible.

Professional procurement's role

In an organisation in which procurement is totally decentralised to the user, the above represents the essential steps which the user should take in order to arrive at a specification of a requirement to meet his or her need.

In organisations where procurement is centralised or centralised/decentralised, the user is the internal customer of the procurement department. It should still be primarily the responsibility of the internal customer to follow the above steps. The professional procurement role is to act in support.

Developing specifications is not easy and the procurement professional should assist an internal customer who is unfamiliar with this sort of work. The first step is to make the internal customer aware of the above process. This might require a short training programme which can be informal if the development of a more straightforward specification is to be done by a single person but might need to be a more formal session with the customary visual aids if the specification is more complex and is to be developed by a team.

All members of the team should understand the process to be followed and, of course, the procurement professional should make sure that he or she is a member of that team. Giving some training at the first meeting of the team is a good way for the procurement professional to establish his or her credentials if there is any doubt among the team members about the role of procurement. If there is no doubt, it does no harm to gently re-emphasise these credentials through a well constructed training brief about the approach discussed above.

During the development of a more complicated specification, the procurement professional will need to support the internal customer and the team. He or she should provide constructive criticism of the specification and make sure that the specification avoids the pitfalls and (very important) that the specification is complete.

This is not easy to do if the procurement professional lacks technical expertise about the product or service to be bought. However, working with the internal customer to develop the specification gives the procurement professional the opportunity to rectify this ignorance. This will strengthen the procurement professional's position during any subsequent work with suppliers, particularly during such stages as supplier selection, negotiation and contract management.

The procurement professional should satisfy him or herself that the commercial information is sound. This information will form the basis of any invitation to tender and/or negotiations and will be used in any subsequent contract. It needs to be as accurate, or at least as realistic, as possible.

CHAPTER 7

Authorisation

Authorisation can occur at various stages of a procurement process. Different persons should authorise each part of the process. There are good reasons for it not being the same person.

The various stages could be:

- budgetary authority;

- authorisation for a procurement process to proceed;

- authorisation for a pre-qualification;

- authorisation of the issue of an invitation to tender or for negotiations to commence;

- authorisation to open tenders;

- authorisation of a contract;

- authorisation or certification of invoices.

Budgetary authority

Budgetary authority is an organisation's way of saying to an individual manager that he or she may use a part of the organisation's resources for some pre-designated purpose. It is a means of dividing up the resources and planning their application in order to achieve the objectives of the organisation. It is not an authority to proceed with a procurement and/or to spend the money without following a recognised and agreed procurement process.

For major purchases, budgets are normally agreed after identification of the need. They are likely to be more accurate if the need has been specified but it is not always practical to specify the need in detail before seeking budgetary approval.

Authorisation of a procurement process

This authorises the procurement process up to the issue of an invitation to tender or negotiate in accordance with the organisation's procurement policy, strategy and procedures. It should follow both the budgetary authority and the steps already described in Chapter 6 to specify the requirement.

The authorisation may be given by the budget holder. It provides an opportunity for the budget holder to ensure that the requirement is still needed, i.e. that the need still exists. However, the budget holder may only authorise procurements of significant value and risk. The authority for other procurements may be delegated to other personnel within the budget holder's department and each department with a budget should have a list of persons who may authorise such procurements. The list should state the limit of each person's financial authority for this purpose. It is the job of the person with this authority to ensure that his or her authority is not exceeded and, most importantly, that that the requirement will really satisfy the need.

Authorisation of a pre-qualification

Pre-qualification is not a cheap process for either the purchasing organisation or for the suppliers who are subjected to it. It needs to be initiated only in cases of real need. To ensure that pre-qualification is not undertaken when it is not appropriate, procurement organisations may wish to give guidance in the procedures about when pre-qualification should be used and to limit the right to authorise a pre-qualification to certain persons in the organisation, for example the head of procurement in an organisation with a centralised procurement structure and appropriate managers in other structures.

Authorisation of the issue of an invitation to tender or to negotiate

This is another aspect where the purchasing organisation may wish to limit to designated individuals the right to authorise the issue of an invitation to tender or to permit negotiations to be conducted. Both of these processes are the preliminaries to a binding contract and it makes sense for the organisation to maintain some control.

Authorisation to open tenders

Tenders should only be opened by persons authorised to open them. The objective is to reduce the risk of any corruption by ensuring that those engaged in the procurement process (the budget holder, the person developing the specification of the requirement, the purchasing agent responsible for the development and issue of the invitation to tender and the person or persons who will ultimately authorise the contract) are not involved in opening tenders.

This process is used more in the public sector and tends to be seen as bureaucratic by those working in the private sector. Although it is not a certain way of avoiding any corruption, it is better than nothing and for this reason it might be worth organisations in the private sector adopting a more formal approach to the opening of tenders.

Authorisation of a contract

This should be covered in the procedures. It is the authorisation to place a contract. The person or persons authorising the contract should be different to the person or persons authorising the procurement process and holding the budget.

Authorisation or certification of invoices

This should be done by somebody other than the person who placed the contract and preferably by somebody not involved in the management of the contract at a detailed level.

CHAPTER 8

Deciding the
procurement approach

In Chapter 5, we discussed the traditional risk–spend matrix and suggested that this was a useful conceptual tool but that it needed to be modified for procurement purposes into a matrix containing five unequal boxes. The boundaries of these boxes depend entirely on what each organisation considers to be best for itself.

In Chapter 6, we discussed how the internal customer must identify the need, define the requirement and develop the specification. The internal customer must also identify the commercial information which is required to buy the requirement. The extent of professional procurement's role depends on the structure of procurement in the organisation, but even where there is centralised procurement, the professional procurement role has mainly a supportive role at this stage.

Assuming that the internal customer has received authorisation of a procurement process, as discussed in Chapter 7, the organisation is now ready to undertake the purchasing activities necessary to obtain the requirement.

If the procurement is of ultra-low spend and low risk, then the process could be undertaken by following a delegated procurement procedure to be described in a later chapter. Ultra-low spend and risk procurements are generally speaking rather obvious and, in many organisations, it is the internal customer who normally undertakes this form of procurement work. Table 8.1 lists who generally undertakes which type of procurement.

Table 8.1 Undertaking the procurement

Type of procurement	Who undertakes
Ultra-low spend	Internal customer
Low spend	Designated persons – possibly not the internal customer
High spend	Trained and qualified procurement agent

Application of the tools and techniques

Other procurement requires more consideration to determine exactly where it fits on a risk–spend matrix. There are a number of tools and techniques which help make these decisions and should be applied by a procurement specialist. These will be discussed later in this chapter. In both the centralised and the centralised/decentralised procurement structures, such procurement specialists will normally exist. In decentralised procurement structures, it is important that there should be some persons who have the skills to apply the tools and techniques.

The procedures should describe the tools and techniques and how they are applied. The procedures should also require their use. This helps to ensure a consistency of approach.

Although many procurement professionals know about these tools and techniques it is doubtful that the tools are applied very much in practice. The usual reasons for this omission are:

- lack of time, particularly if the internal customer wants the requirement urgently; and

- the belief held by a lot of procurement professionals that they can achieve what the tools and techniques would achieve but without the hassle of using them.

In fact, using the tools and techniques is not a lot of extra work and they do ensure a thorough analysis which should lead to better decisions. By enabling an early and objective assessment of the procurement and the circumstances surrounding it, the tools and techniques should ensure that the best procurement approach is adopted. If the conclusion arising from their use contradicts a procurement practitioner's instinct, then this should be explored to see why.

It is not unreasonable for an organisation to expect procurement professionals to know about the tools and their use. This argues for knowledgeable procurement professionals being retained by all organisations irrespective of whether they have a centralised, centralised/decentralised or decentralised structure.

Purchase of low-spend, low-risk requirements

We have said above that ultra-low procurements should be undertaken by the internal customer. It is important that the procedures make this clear. Equally, they should make it clear that other low-spend procurements, which might be a higher spend than the ultra-low value ones but are still low-spend and low-risk procurements, might also be undertaken on a delegated basis without extensive analysis once they have been identified.

The procedures should require that procurements over a certain spend value must be undertaken by a different person to the internal customer. This person should be somebody who cannot be influenced by the internal customer. Separation of the roles of the person with the need from the person with the authority to buy is important to avoid fraud.

Assessing risk and total spend

The first step is for the person who will be doing the procurement (for whom we use the term *procurement agent* from now on) to examine the specification and the commercial information provided by the internal customer (see Figure 8.1). If the procurement agent has been involved in the consultative role mentioned in Chapter 6, then this might be unnecessary. If the procurement agent has some reservations about either the specification or the commercial information, now is the time for this to be raised with the internal customer.

Steps for procurement agent to follow:

1. Examine the specification and commercial information.

2. Discuss any concerns with the internal customer.

3. Ascertain opportunities for consolidation.

4. Review risk and resolve any differences of opinion with internal customer.

5. Calculate likely total spend.

Figure 8.1 Steps for procurement agent to follow.

The procurement agent should now ascertain whether there are any opportunities for consolidation of the requirement with other similar requirements in order to obtain possible advantages of scale when purchasing. This applies to the purchase of both goods and services.

The internal customer should have provided some assessment of the risk of the procurement. The procurement agent should review this and, if he or she disagrees and it is not possible for the procurement agent and the internal customer to reconcile their differing views, then the matter should be submitted to a third party, usually somebody senior to the two people in disagreement. The procedures should specify whom and, in organisations with a head of procurement, it would normally be this person.

The procedures should require the procurement agent to calculate the likely total spend over the lifetime of this procurement.

It might be helpful to give guidance about how this might be done although a procurement professional should have no difficulty in undertaking this activity.

Plotting the risk–spend matrix

The procurement agent now has a total spend and a measure of the risk. He or she should now be able to plot the proposed procurement onto the risk–spend matrix. Now that the ultra-low spend procurement has been assigned for purchase by the internal customer, the plotting could be, if preferred, on the four-box matrix provided that the boundaries between the boxes has been agreed. It is helpful for these boundaries to be specified in the procedures.

The matrix (reproduced in Figure 8.2) indicates an approach to be applied to any procurement falling in a given box. In Chapter 5, we defined these as follows:

- *High risk/high spend* – manage the relationship for optimum procurement results.

- *Low risk/high spend* – look for profitable procurement opportunities.

- *High risk/low spend* – protect.

- *Low risk/low spend* – minimise the work but protect the organisation.

Thus the position of this procurement on the matrix gives the procurement agent a guide about the approach to the procurement.

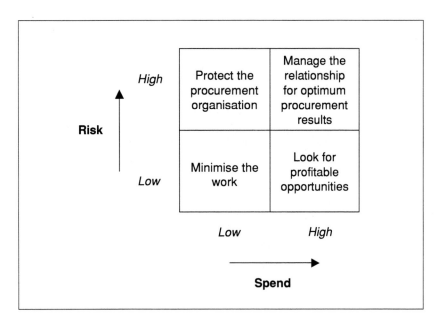

Figure 8.2 Risk–spend matrix.

The procedures now need to describe other tools which will refine the procurement approach and give greater assurance that the best approach is being adopted. It is not suggested that these tools should be applied to every procurement irrespective of value and risk. There is probably little point in applying them to low-risk, low-spend procurement which, in terms of numbers of purchases, is likely to be the majority. The procedures should give the procurement agent the discretion not to apply these tools to such procurements and we have already discussed how the procedures may specify who should deal with them. However, for the other types of procurement, there is merit in applying the tools and procurement agents should be encouraged to do so.

The various tools are described below.

The customer positioning portfolio

The customer positioning portfolio is the vendor's way of looking at the marketplace because it may give the vendor an indication of the best sales/marketing approach to be adopted. It can be used by procurement organisations to predict possible sales/marketing strategies of different suppliers with respect to a particular procurement.

Figure 8.3 shows the customer positioning portfolio. Note that the two axes are 'Likelihood of future business from the procurement organisation' and 'Relative amount of current business from the procurement organisation'.

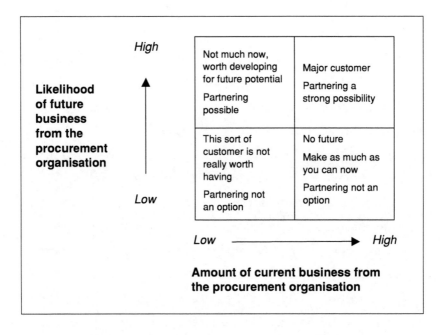

Figure 8.3 Customer positioning portfolio.

The procedures should require the procurement agent to plot the procurement onto the customer positioning portfolio. To do this the procurement agent must identify possible sources of supply. At this stage the procurement agent does not know whether any of these vendors will be the ultimate supplier to the organisation.

It is useful to plot a range of suppliers, both large and small, because the procurement organisation's spend might be small to large suppliers and large to smaller suppliers.

Over a period of time, the demand for the requirement might grow or it might remain static or it might fall. It might be a one-off purchase. This commercial information should have been identified by the internal customer, so the procurement agent can assess whether the business with the supplier is likely to grow or not, i.e. the procurement agent can assess where the procurement will fall on the vertical axis of the portfolio.

The spend value of the procurement should be evaluated against each supplier's likely sales revenue for this type of requirement. This can be difficult to ascertain. It is usually easier to establish the vendor's total sales revenue (from its accounts) and compare the spend value of the requirement with the sales revenue. This gives an assessment of the relative importance of the spend to the vendor. This is the horizontal axis in Figure 8.3.

Although the customer positioning portfolio identifies possible sales/marketing strategies for each potential vendor, it does not follow that the vendor will adopt this approach. The portfolio, like the risk–spend matrix, is only a model and it might not be a true reflection of reality. However, it gives food for thought when planning a contract strategy. If the risk–spend matrix is suggesting that the procurement should be managed for optimum results but the customer positioning portfolio is suggesting that the vendor's view might be that the procurement organisation is not worth having as a customer, then there is an obvious mismatch which could mean that a partnering approach, usually advocated for high-risk/high-spend procurements, is probably going to be difficult to obtain in practice.

It is instructive if each of the boxes in the risk–spend matrix is compared with the boxes in the customer positioning portfolio. For example, assume that a procurement falls in the high-risk/high-spend box in the risk–spend matrix. What might happen if this procurement were to fall in the 'Major customer' box in the customer positioning portfolio? It is obviously in both organisations' interest to have a partnering style relationship and this sort of relationship should be a real possibility. Partnering might also be possible if the procurement fell in the 'Not much now, worth developing' box on the customer positioning portfolio. However, partnering might be more difficult if the procurement fell in either of the two bottom boxes. In the bottom right, the supplier is interested in making money by treating this procurement as a cash cow – hardly the attitude which leads to a partnering relationship. In the bottom left, there might be no interest in selling to the procurement organisation.

The reader should repeat this process by comparing each box in the risk–spend matrix with all four of the boxes in the customer positioning portfolio.

If there are other procurements which are made from a supplier in this marketplace, this needs to be taken into account when considering the customer positioning portfolio. For example, a supplier which already classifies a procurement organisation as a major customer will be more likely to be a good supplier of anything falling in the bottom two boxes.

The customer positioning portfolio depicts a likely point of view of the supplier with respect to a particular procurement. Understanding it helps the procurement agent to stand in the shoes of the supplier and see the marketplace and the potential relationship with the procurement organisation from the point of view of the supplier.

The objective is to check whether the procurement approach suggested by the risk–spend matrix is likely to be sustainable in practice.

While it is theoretically desirable to apply the customer positioning portfolio to all procurements other than the ultra-low spend, it will be a lot of work to apply it to all low-risk/low-spend procurements. If this is the case, the procedures should make it clear that procurements of this type should be treated differently and the customer positioning portfolio need not be applied to them.

It is also important to note that the suppliers plotted on the customer positioning portfolio do not need, at this stage, to have been pre-qualified. Simple identification is enough. It can be that the use of this matrix will give some clue about which suppliers should be considered for pre-qualification. The conclusions drawn from using the matrix should, of course, be verified during the pre-qualification process. Pre-qualification is discussed in a later chapter.

The purchasing power line

The purchasing power line is just a horizontal line on a piece of paper, one end of which represents 100 per cent power to the purchasing organisation and 0 per cent to the supplier and the other represents 100 per cent power to the supplier and 0 per cent power to the purchasing organisation (see Figure 8.4).

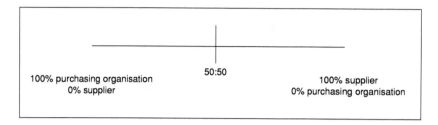

Figure 8.4 The purchasing power line.

Table 8.2, based loosely on Porter's Five Forces, assists in deciding where the power lies.

Table 8.2 Deciding where the power lies

Factor	Buyer will have the most power when	Supplier will have the most power when
1	Supplier's capacity exceeds demand.	Buyer's demand exceeds supply.
2	It is easy for new suppliers to enter the market.	It is difficult for new suppliers to enter the market.
3	Switching costs are low.	Switching costs are high.
4	Other products can be used instead of the one being bought.	Only the supplier's product will do.

Factor	Buyer will have the most power when	Supplier will have the most power when
5	It is easy to find new suppliers at home or abroad.	It is difficult to find new suppliers, perhaps no new suppliers exist.
6	Buyer buys a lot as a percentage of supplier's total business.	Buyer does not buy much as a percentage of supplier's total business.
7	Buyer is an attractive customer to the supplier, for example because the buyer's demand is growing, there is some kudos in supplying the buyer and/or there is no hassle in dealing with the buyer because the buyer pays on time and/or the buyer does not cancel or change orders, etc.	The buyer is not an attractive customer, for example because the buyer's demand is static or falling and other customers' demand is growing, there is no kudos, the buyer is a lot of hassle to deal with.

A scoring system is used. A maximum of ten points is allowed for each factor and they are distributed between the buyer and the supplier. For example, if the capacity of all the suppliers in the market significantly exceeds the demand, then the buyer side might score 8 and the supplier side 2. If it is quite difficult for new suppliers to enter the market, the supplier side might score 7 and the buyer side 3. If switching costs are high, the supplier side might score 9 and the buyer side 1. And so on, until each factor has been scored. Add up the buyer's points and express as a percentage of 70. Plot the position of this percentage on the purchasing power line. This gives an indication of the power which the procurement organisation has with respect to a supplier.

The procurement agent must use his or her judgement when scoring and must undertake reasonable research to reach the best possible conclusion.

If the procurement organisation has the power in the relationship, it can use it to influence matters to its advantage.

The procedures should require the procurement agent to use the purchasing power line to assess which party is likely to be more powerful in the market.

Partnering

The results from using the above tools should indicate whether there is any possibility of having a partnering relationship with a supplier.

It also helps if the procurement organisation has more power than a possible supplier as the procurement organisation can take the lead in any partnering relationship. Even in partnering relationships, the procurement organisation and the supplier are, in power terms, seldom in a relationship between equals.

If the supplier has the power, then partnering is only possible if the supplier wants it. Indications from the risk–spend matrix and the customer positioning portfolio might suggest that circumstances are propitious for a partnering relationship but this does not mean that the supplier will want this sort of relationship.

When considering the possibility of a partnering relationship, the procedures should require the procurement agent to take into account the characteristics of a partnering relationship. These characteristics are:

- shared objectives – there has to be a win-win situation;

- trust – which takes time to build;

- openness and honesty – obviously dependent on trust existing;

- good communications – these should not be left to chance but should be designed into the relationship;

- proactive problem-solving;

- sharing of risk and rewards – usually taken to mean that the partner best able to manage the risk accepts it;

- willingness to engage in continuous performance improvement;

- willingness to engage in continuous cost reduction;

- pooling of knowledge and resources;

- mutual learning;

- existence in both the procurement organisation and the supplier of the right culture for partnering;

- trained staff with the right attitude to partnering.

In particular, partnering relationships embody the following characteristics:

- Recognition of the other party's objectives. Both parties have their own objectives. Each party recognises the other's objectives and works with the other party to ensure that it meets them. The procurement organisation's objective is the successful delivery of supplies, services or works. Successful means the delivery of what the procurement organisation has defined as value. It will mean the delivery of the desired or right supplies, services or works delivered on time, at the right cost, to the right place, at the right quality (the five 'rights'). The supplier wishes to be adequately rewarded for the supplies, services or works which it delivers. Provided such rewards are strictly in compliance with the contract, the procurement organisation must not impede payment to the supplier. The supplier may have other objectives, such as enhancing its reputation as a sound supplier, provided these are legal and do not jeopardise the procurement organisation. They should also not be impeded.

- Both parties are committed to the success of the contract as this is the best way for both parties to achieve their objectives. Consequently, both parties seek to work with one another in a close and mutually helpful way to deliver the objectives of the contract.

- Open, honest communication and trust are key factors which lead to the success of a partnering contract. This normally involves open book accounting by both parties.

- Both parties exhibit high standards of ethical behaviour. There must be transparency in all dealings.

- Both parties see themselves as joint members of a team seeking to deliver the contract's objectives as well as meeting the objectives of both parties. Each party is focused on the ultimate customer.

- Instead of an adversarial 'we win, you lose' approach both parties dedicate themselves to win-win outcomes whereby each party gains something of benefit.

- Both parties employ total quality management to meet their goals. Their leadership style is participative and they avoid a blame culture.

If it is apparent that many of the above criteria are not likely to be satisfied, the procurement agent should consider whether a partnering arrangement is likely to be a practical and successful relationship.

Partnering is a form of procurement which has led to significantly improved performance at much lower cost. It is also a form of procurement which has had its failures and these tend to be more damaging than normal commercial relationships. Partnering is demanding of an organisation's resources. It is not only the procurement agent or the department responsible for procurement which has to manage and cope with all the work associated with partnering. The internal customer department and other departments can be heavily engaged. So it is right that the procedures should require early consideration of the possibility of partnering and set clear guidelines for identifying likely partnering opportunities.

If a relationship is not fit for partnering, then a usual commercial relationship will apply. Even here, there is a whole spectrum ranging from adversarial to amicable and cooperative. The preceding analysis of power and how potential suppliers may see the relationship provides a useful insight as to what sort of relationship might exist. It also tells the procurement agent whether the procurement organisation is likely to be in a strong or weak bargaining position in an eventual relationship.

Measurement of supplier performance

Measurement of supplier performance is also something which should be considered at this stage. It is often not considered at all or considered after a contract is let.

It is something which should be discussed with the internal customer whose need is to be satisfied by the supplier.

For many procurements, performance is straightforward and can be defined in simple quality and delivery terms. These are not likely to be the subject of protracted discussion between the procurement agent and the internal customer. However, for more complex procurements including partnering, supplier performance can be a much more involved affair and the sooner it is considered the better. This permits it to be built into any invitation to tender and into the contract.

CHAPTER 9

Supplier appraisal: pre-qualification and qualification

Supplier appraisal

As with many aspects of procurement, 'supplier appraisal' is a term which can have more than one meaning. It may mean just pre-qualification on its own. It may also mean both pre-qualification and qualification.

It may mean supplier performance measurement which is also called supplier rating or vendor rating. It may also be used as a generic to include all of these activities some of which (pre-qualification and qualification) take place before a contract is let and some of which (supplier performance measurement) take place after the letting of a contract.

It is the generic use which is adopted in this book and to make it clear which type of supplier appraisal is meant, the words pre-qualification, qualification or supplier performance measurement will also be used as appropriate.

Pre-qualification

Pre-qualification is a process to determine the acceptability of possible suppliers. Suppliers should only be deemed acceptable if they are potentially able to supply whatever is required by the procurement organisation. Usually, this means that they are able to supply the requirements as specified (i.e. to the right specification), at the right quality, to the right place, at the right time and at the right cost.

Summary:

- Supplier appraisal can mean pre-qualification, qualification or supplier performance measurement.

- Pre-qualification is a process to determine the acceptability of possible suppliers.

- Approved suppliers list (ASL): pre-qualified suppliers are added to the approved suppliers list.

- Qualification is the selection for tendering purposes of suppliers from the ASL.

The supplier must have certain attributes to meet the five 'rights' consistently. Pre-qualification is a way of checking that the supplier has these attributes. Of course, even if a supplier has all of the attributes, there can be procurement difficulties, for example the supplier may not want to supply the procurement organisation. An examination of the customer positioning portfolio and the purchasing power line, both discussed in the previous chapter, should give some useful guidance about this.

Pre-qualification is not an infallible tool; rather it is a risk reduction exercise which helps identify those suppliers which do not have the attributes to supply consistently. Preferably, such suppliers should be avoided or used providing the risk of using them can be properly managed. If avoidance is not possible, the procurement organisation can use pre-qualification to assess what the future difficulties might be. Forewarned is forearmed and the procurement agent might be able to take steps to mitigate a possible supply disaster.

The outcome of pre-qualification is a list of suppliers for any category of spend which should be good suppliers. Pre-qualification is undertaken when the requirement has been specified and the commercial information is available. For repeat requirements, there will probably be a list of approved suppliers. However, new suppliers, with which the procurement organisation has previously had no dealings, may request to be pre-qualified and added to the list. There could also be circumstances where the procurement organisation is dissatisfied with the suppliers which have been pre-qualified and wishes to add to its list by pre-qualifying a supplier with which it has not previously dealt.

Lists of approved suppliers have various names: approved suppliers list and preferred suppliers list are both very common. Often these are abbreviated to ASL and PSL. In this book, the term approved suppliers list will be used.

Procurement organisations with such lists normally have rules which forbid the use of suppliers which are not on the list. Such rules should, of course, be stated in the procedures.

Qualification

Most procurement organisations subscribe to the view that they should test the market from time to time in order to stimulate competition and hopefully to gain some advantage from it. To stimulate competition they will need to select suppliers from their approved list and approach them for bids for the business which the procurement organisation has to offer. This selection process is known as *qualification*. It is a form of mini pre-qualification which is used if there are far more suppliers on the approved suppliers list than are needed in order to stimulate competition in a cost-effective manner.

The objective of qualification is firstly to check whether there has been any change in the facts established about any supplier during the pre-qualification. This is most important if the suppliers have been on the approved list for some time but have not been given any business so that contact with them has been limited. There could have been changes in their circumstances which mean that the information gained during the pre-qualification process and the conclusions drawn from it are no longer valid. Possibly, the previously pre-qualified supplier is no longer eligible to be on the approved suppliers list.

Another purpose of qualification is to establish that a supplier is interested in supplying and has the free capacity and resources available to do so. A supplier which had all the necessary capacity and resources, such as equipment, suitably qualified personnel, financial resources, business systems, etc. when it was pre-qualified might no longer have any free capacity or resources. All of the supplier's capacity and resources could be fully occupied in supplying other clients. Self-evidently, there is little point in approaching suppliers in these circumstances.

Explanation in the procedures

A procurement organisation should consider the extent to which it wishes to discuss in its procedures the issues mentioned above about the nature of pre-qualification and qualification. If the procedures are seen as an educative tool, then some discussion would be merited but this could be part of the training associated with the launch of the procedures.

Identifying potential suppliers

For new categories of spend or for categories of spend where there appear to be few or no suppliers, the procurement agent will need to research the market to identify suppliers prior to undertaking pre-qualification and qualification (see Figure 9.1). This might need to be done as part of work to define the requirement if the internal customer does not have the expertise to define the need and it is felt necessary to request information from potential suppliers (see Chapter 6).

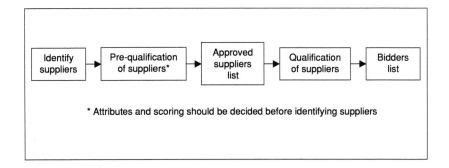

Figure 9.1 Process: identification of suppliers to bidders list.

The procedures should give guidance about where to look rather than how a search for suppliers should be undertaken. A list of the following sort could be included:

- directories such as Kompass, Kelly's and Sells;

- searches on the Internet;

- trade magazines – sometimes the editorial staff might be able to help, and back issues of the magazines may be worth scanning for articles and advertisements;

- trade bodies;

- existing suppliers – an innocent remark such as 'there does not seem to be many suppliers in this or that market' can yield results;

- competitors – worth a try as they might be willing to tell you something or let something slip, and are often worth trying when at conferences, exhibitions, etc.;

- other likely purchasers of goods and services – think who might want to buy the goods or services which you want, contact them and see if they will share their information;

- historical records – your own records can help;

- for purchases from abroad – there is often staff at the embassy who have responsibility for helping you find sources of supply. They might be able to recommend trade directories but these could be in their language not English. The Internet can also be a source of information.

Nowadays, the most popular source of information about new suppliers is the Internet.

Managing a pre-qualification

The first step is to decide whether full pre-qualification is necessary or not. A full pre-qualification is an expensive exercise and should not be applied to every procurement. The adaptation of the four-box risk–spend matrix shown in Figure 9.2 makes this plain.

The procedures should require a full pre-qualification of any supplier of the categories of goods and services which fall in Box 3 as the risk and spend are both high.

For categories of spend falling into Box 4, it is not unusual to find that there are few suppliers for this type of requirement. If the numbers are very small, pre-qualification is often nothing more than an information-gathering exercise for these suppliers.

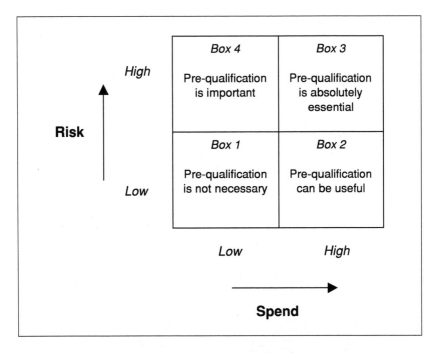

Figure 9.2 Adapting the risk–spend matrix
to manage pre-qualification.

For Box 2, there are often a large number of suppliers available and pre-qualification is often used to reduce this number to something more manageable.

Suppliers falling into Box 4 are normally pre-qualified over the telephone or by e-mail by obtaining answers to a few simple questions. This applies, of course, to the majority of suppliers.

In any box, the pre-qualification will need to be tailored to the category of spend. The objective of the procedure is to set a template which is adapted by the procurement agent. The most helpful approach is to describe a full pre-qualification applicable to categories falling in Box 3 and then leave it to the discretion of the procurement agent to tailor the full approach to meet the needs of each of the other boxes. However, it needs to be stressed that tailoring will also be required for spends falling in Box 3.

The first step is to list the supplier attributes which might be reviewed during the pre-qualification. The following would be included:

- technical capability to supply;

- financial stability;

- available capacity;

- quality capability;

- delivery capability;

- industrial relations record;

- quality of management;

- culture of the organisation;

- research facilities;

- existing customer satisfaction;

- approach to partnering;

- cost structure;

- capability to trade electronically;

- ability to cope with urgent demands;

- IT capability;

- environmental considerations;

- health and safety considerations;

- fair trade considerations.

Not all attributes would need examination for every procurement falling in Box 3. For the other boxes, the above list might need quite drastic tailoring to make it suitable. The procedures should make it clear that it is the procurement agent's responsibility to undertake this tailoring by consulting with appropriate colleagues to determine the right mix of attributes.

It is necessary to define what each attribute means and how it could be measured. This is not easy as many of the attributes are softer issues. The procedures should make it clear that the procurement agent should work with appropriate colleagues to define each required attribute and to develop the most objective measuring approach. The procedures should not specify in detail how this should be done on an attribute by attribute basis. It is quite possible that a different definition and measuring approach will be needed for the same attribute when applied to suppliers of different goods and services. The procedures should be restricted to a statement that this work should be done and that it is the responsibility of the procurement agent to see that it is done and the responsibility of other personnel to participate and help as required.

The procedures also need to make it clear that the procurement agent should work with colleagues to develop a scoring system for each of the selected and defined attributes.

A possible approach is to score each attribute out of some suitable total score, say 100. It might be that the points should be distributed around the various components of an attribute. For example, financial stability might be determined on the basis of a supplier's cash flow, profitability, current ratio and debt/equity gearing (these measures are not recommended as the only measures – they are used for illustration only). Cash flow might, with some justification, be seen as the most important measure and awarded 40 points as a maximum score. Each of the other attributes might be awarded a maximum of 20 points each. Each of these components might now be scored and the individual scores added to give a total score for financial stability out of 100.

Another important step is for the procurement agent and appropriate colleagues to decide a pass/fail mark for each attribute. For example, an organisation's technical ability to supply is usually extremely important and a high pass mark, say 80, should be set. On the other hand, an ability to cope with urgent demands might not be so important, so a lower pass mark, say 40, could be set.

The importance of setting a pass mark for each attribute is that a supplier fails the pre-qualification as a whole if it does not exceed the pass mark for an attribute and as some attributes are more important to the procurement organisation than others, the pass mark should be set higher for them.

It is also necessary to set a weighting for each attribute. The maximum weighting might be 5 and the minimum might be 1. The more important the attribute the higher the weighting.

During the pre-qualification, a score is assigned for each attribute. Any failures to pass would mean automatic disqualification of the supplier. The score for an attribute is multiplied by the weighting for that attribute to arrive at a weighted score. The weighted scores for all the attributes are added together and the suppliers are ranked in descending order of total weighted scores.

During the pre-qualification, all attributes are scored. Any failure to exceed the pass/fail mark for an attribute would mean automatic disqualification of the supplier. For those suppliers which have not been disqualified in this way, the score for each attribute is multiplied by the weighting for that attribute to arrive at a weighted score. The weighted scores for all the attributes are added together and the suppliers are ranked in descending order of total weighted scores.

There needs to be a pass/fail mark for total weighted scores. All suppliers exceeding this pass/fail weighted score have been approved. The weightings are very important as, without them, it would be possible to have an approved list consisting of suppliers with high scores in not so important attributes but low scores in more important attributes.

An outline of the scoring process is provided in Figure 9.3. Note that decisions about scoring should be made before engaging in any activity with a supplier. For preference, they should be made before suppliers have been identified as this prevents contact with suppliers from influencing the process.

Decisions about attributes and their scores should be made in consultation with the internal customer.

The procedures should also require the procurement agent to decide how the information needed from each supplier should be obtained. Normally, it is obtained either by making a visit to the supplier or by issuing a questionnaire. There might also be an interview of key personnel from suppliers who might be asked to make a presentation and answer questions. Sometimes, there is a stage approach; for example, a questionnaire is issued, suppliers make presentations and a visit is made. The information pertinent to an attribute is gathered from this process and then scored.

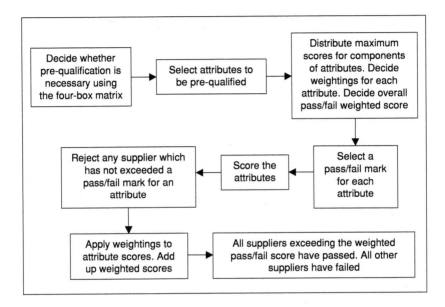

Figure 9.3 Outline of scoring process for supplier qualification.

There is little point in the procedures stipulating in detail how the information should be gathered. What is needed is a requirement for the procurement agent to work with colleagues to come up with a cost-effective (remember pre-qualification can be very expensive for both the procurement organisation and the potential supplier) and appropriate approach which might well differ from category to category of spend.

The procedures should require any evaluation and scoring to be fair and reasonable. They should also require a clear audit trail to be made. This helps counter complaints about unfairness which are made from time to time and they also help ensure avoidance of fraud by making it difficult for anybody to manipulate the approved suppliers list without it being detectable.

Organisations in the public and utilities sectors are required by law to disclose to potential suppliers the evaluation and scoring systems which are to be used. This is not a bad practice. Some procurement practitioners fear that this will give a potential supplier an opportunity to disguise the truth about any attribute. This is possible but it is also possible that it will give the supplier the opportunity to present pertinent information for the evaluation.

Managing qualification

The outcome of pre-qualification is a list of approved suppliers which should be maintained by the procurement department in organisations with a centralised or centralised/decentralised structure. For organisations which are totally decentralised, the list will have to be maintained by the person responsible for each procurement, although some thought should be given to having the list maintained centrally, possibly by the audit department or by the company secretary.

Qualification is the process of selecting suppliers from the approved list for the purpose of inviting them to make offers to supply goods or services, whether this is done by tendering or through negotiation.

The procedures should require the procurement agent to develop fair and reasonable criteria for selecting suppliers. The procedures should not specify what these criteria are although it might make suggestions by way of example. Possibilities are:

- the length of time suppliers have been on the list – the preference should be to select the longest;

- the likelihood a particular supplier can supply the requirement – theoretically, all pre-qualified suppliers should be able to supply the requirement, although special circumstances may mean that some suppliers are better able to supply than others;

- past or current performance.

It is normal for existing suppliers to be put on any list of suppliers for inviting tenders or negotiation provided these suppliers have performed satisfactorily.

The procedures should require the procurement agent to check that the suppliers are still willing to supply and that there have been no substantial changes since pre-qualification if this was conducted some time ago.

Finally, the procedures should require an audit trail to ensure that the qualification process has been conducted properly and to minimise the possibility of fraud.

CHAPTER 10

Procurement practices

This chapter deals with the practice of procurement for each of the following:

- supplies, services and works (i.e. construction of civil structures or their maintenance) of high spend (Boxes 1 and 2 in Figure 10.1);

- supplies, services and works of low spend and high risk (Box 3 in Figure 10.1);

- supplies, services and works of low spend and low risk (Box 4 in Figure 10.1);

- small-spend procurement, i.e. supplies, services and works whose consolidated spend is ultra low (Box 5 in Figure 10.1).

(Figure 10.1 reproduces Figure 5.2 and was discussed in detail in Chapter 5.)

The boundaries in this particular model are not defined and it is for each organisation to define its own.

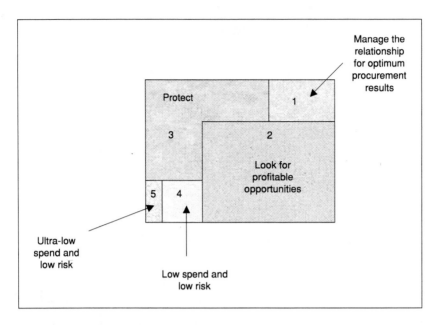

Figure 10.1 Risk–spend matrix.

For all these procurements, the procedures should deal with the need to use pre-qualification, qualification, tendering or negotiation. The former two have been previously discussed and the latter two will be discussed in later chapters.

The spends referred to below are fully consolidated spends over a period such as a year. In some instances this might not be known, in which case it will need to be estimated or guessed (and, of course, the guess needs to be a reasonable one).

Supplies, services and works of high spend (Boxes 1 and 2)

For procurements with a high spend there should be a contract strategy which should be produced by the procurement agent in consultation with the internal customer and other specialists, for example legal and financial, as necessary.

The procedures should require the contract strategy to be a written document dealing with some or all of the following:

- type of contract, e.g. partnering, framework agreement, single contract, purchase order, design and build;

- terms and conditions to be used;

- duration of contract in years;

- demand each year of the contract for whatever is being procured;

- amount likely to be spent each year of the proposed contract;

- anticipated whole-life cost;

- number of suppliers to receive contracts, i.e. whether there is to be multiple sourcing;

- number of potential suppliers to be invited to tender or participate in any negotiation;

- subcontract arrangements;

- approach to letting the contract, e.g. by invitation to tender or, exceptionally, by negotiation;

- tender evaluation criteria and methodology;

- process to be followed to obtain approval for the letting of the contract;

- where the power in any subsequent relationship is likely to lie – the purchasing power line can be used to understand this;

- who will manage the contract when it has been let and how this management will be accomplished so that the organisation is not exposed to any commercial risk;

- what crucial milestones are to be included in any contract;

- how supplier performance will be measured.

The purpose of this document is to encourage forward thinking and the procedures should describe an approval structure depending on the likely value of the contract. In centralised structures, the person responsible for approving should be the head of procurement. In centralised/decentralised structures, it could be the head of procurement or some person in the decentralised part of the organisation. In decentralised organisations, a person will have to be nominated.

In addition, the procurement agent should list all the activities necessary to let a contract in the form of a timetabled contract plan. The plan should consider the following as appropriate and be agreed with the internal customer:

- receipt of specification and of the authorisation for a procurement process;

- completion of the strategy;

- development of the ITT;

- approval of the ITT;

- pre-qualification of suppliers;

- qualification of suppliers;

- issue of the ITT or invitation to negotiate;

- return of tenders or start of negotiations;

- completion of evaluation of tenders or completion of negotiations;

- completion of any written recommendation to place a contract;

- approval of the recommendation to place a contract;

- letting the contract;

- first delivery of the supplies or services or commencement of work in the case of works or services.

The procedures should require consideration to be given to the possibility of a partnering relationship, especially for spend falling into Box 1. However, there is no need to be slavish about this and spends falling into Box 2 could also be eligible for a partnering relationship (see Figure 10.2). The factors for deciding whether a partnering relationship is appropriate have been discussed in a previous chapter.

The procedures should require any partnering relationships to be based on legally binding contracts in writing and for suppliers in such relationships to be selected using the pre-qualification and qualification processes previously described.

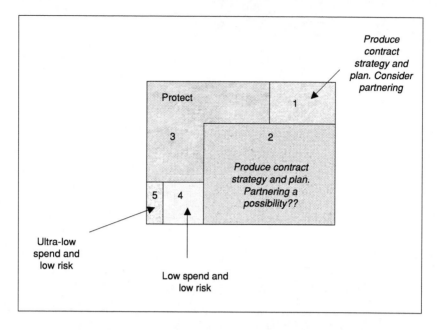

Figure 10.2 Considering the possiblity of partnership.

As has been previously discussed, the procedures should also make it clear that value and not price is to be the determining factor of contract award.

Supplies, services and works of low spend and high risk (Box 3)

The requirement here is for the procurement agent to explore ways of minimising risk (see Figure 10.3). Possibilities include the following:

- buying sufficient quantities to be attractive to suppliers and holding stock (applies to supplies only);

- letting contracts whose duration is sufficiently long to be of interest to suppliers (may apply to supplies, services and works of the maintenance sort);

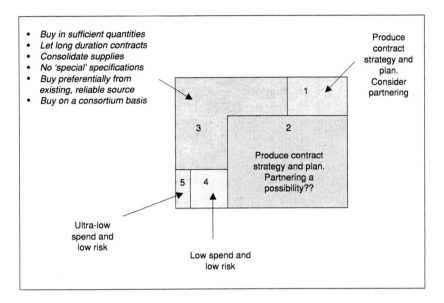

Figure 10.3 Minimising risk.

- consolidating the supply of the low-spend/high-risk requirement with a high-risk/high-spend requirement or a low-risk/high-spend requirement which might be of greater interest to a prospective supplier and letting one contract to the supplier for the supply of both requirements. This effectively links the supply of the more attractive requirement with the less attractive requirement (may apply to supplies, services and works);

- examining the specification to ensure that the high-risk/low-spend requirement is not unnecessarily 'special'. Another requirement might meet the need and this requirement might fall into other boxes on the matrix. The internal customer must assist with this examination (may apply to supplies, services and works);

- buying preferentially from an established and reliable source (may apply to supplies, services and works);

- seeking to buy the item on a consortium basis with other organisations (may apply to supplies, services and works). There will need to be a written contractual arrangement with the other organisations in the consortium and any liability of the procurement organisation should be minimised and/or be commensurate with the risk involved if the item were not supplied.

Other approaches to minimise risk may be available depending on the circumstances at the time. The procedures should grant the procurement agent the flexibility to investigate all possibilities and adopt the best available.

The procedures need to define who should approve the arrangement to minimise risk.

Supplies, services and works of low spend and low risk (Box 4)

The object for this type of procurement is to find a balance between minimising the amount spent and minimising the transaction cost (see Figure 10.4).

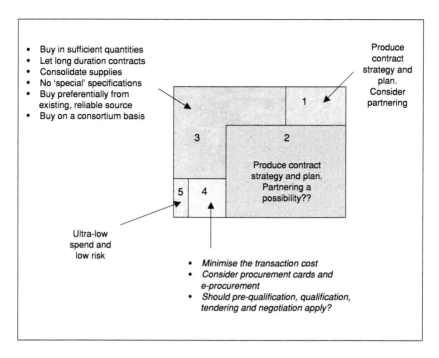

- Buy in sufficient quantities
- Let long duration contracts
- Consolidate supplies
- No 'special' specifications
- Buy preferentially from existing, reliable source
- Buy on a consortium basis

Produce contract strategy and plan. Consider partnering

1

3

2

Produce contract strategy and plan. Partnering a possibility??

5 4

Ultra-low spend and low risk

- *Minimise the transaction cost*
- *Consider procurement cards and e-procurement*
- *Should pre-qualification, qualification, tendering and negotiation apply?*

Figure 10.4 Ways of minimising transaction costs for Box 4 procurements.

The procedures should require procurement cards or e-procurement methods to be used for this type of procurement if these tools are available.

The procedures might also require pre-qualification, qualification, tendering and negotiation to apply but discretion should be permitted to the procurement agent to adapt these so that the work involved is not excessive, i.e. so that the transaction cost is kept as low as possible commensurate with a reasonable procurement good practice.

It is particularly important that the procedures require an audit trail.

Small-spend procurement – supplies, services and works whose consolidated spend is ultra low (Box 5)

The prime objective is to minimise the transaction cost of procurement.

It is also important that there is an adequate audit trail to prevent dishonesty. A way of doing this is to specify what records of the transaction should be kept, for example:

- a copy of the specification used and reasons why it was chosen;

- how many suppliers were invited to offer prices and why they were selected and what terms and conditions have been agreed;

- the original quotations from suppliers;

- a copy of the order or contract which has been placed;

- the reason why the order or contract has been placed with a particular supplier;

- copies of any correspondence about the procurement;

- copies of any goods received notes;

- copies of invoices;

- any other notes necessary to ensure a satisfactory audit trail.

The procedures should also deal with the following:

- the permissibility of using a supplier's catalogue number to specify what is required – this is often very convenient for this type of procurement;

- recognition that the terms and conditions which will be used are most likely going to be the supplier's. Irrespective of the structure of procurement in the organisation, this sort of procurement is often either delegated to junior staff or undertaken by staff with no understanding of the contract law principles underpinning terms and conditions. Rules that 'all procurement must be done on our terms and conditions' are unlikely to be observed in practice;

- recognition that the procurement is quite possibly going to be done over the telephone or by e-mail – it is prudent to require that confirmation is given in writing;

- recognition that for ultra-low spend procurement, there is little point in seeking bids from more than one supplier.

Procurement cards and e-procurement can also be used for procurements of this type.

CHAPTER 11

Tendering and negotiation

The aspects to be considered in this chapter are restricted and open tendering, single- and sole-source tendering and negotiation.

Restricted tendering means that the number of suppliers to be invited to tender is restricted to a selection from those available through the pre-qualification and qualification procedures. Often a minimum and maximum number to be invited to tender may be specified in procedures although these might be varied in special circumstances.

Open tendering occurs when the procurement organisation invites supplier organisations to request an invitation to tender. The request is usually made by means of an advertisement in the press, trade journals or on a website. All of the suppliers requesting an invitation will be given one and each of them may submit a tender. The procurement organisation does not try to limit the number of bids in any way. There is no pre-qualification or qualification procedure applied.

Sole-source tendering is when there is a sole source of supply, i.e. the supplier is a monopoly. In some cases, this is because the procurement organisation effectively confers monopoly status on the supplier, for example when it is decided to use only a certain artist to paint a picture of the chairman of the board. If no other artist will do, then the chosen artist obviously has a monopoly. It is to be hoped that artistic tastes are sufficiently broad in procurement organisations that several artists could be invited to bid.

Single-source tendering occurs when a procurement organisation chooses to seek a tender from one source only when there are other sources available which could tender if invited to do so. The only really valid reasons for single sourcing are urgency and integration. Integration occurs when the procurement organisation already possesses some asset, such as computer software or capital equipment, and it is necessary to integrate in some way whatever is now being bought with that asset. Difficulties and expense would arise if some other equipment were bought. Other sources are available but the procurement seeks to minimise cost and effort by sticking with the existing source.

Tendering and negotiation are sometimes seen as being rivals. In fact, they are two tools which can be used to great effect independently of one or another or complementarily. To absolutely reject the use of one is to reduce the tools in the procurement tool kit and to use one rather than the other on the basis of personal preference is just self-indulgence. Whether one should be used in place of the other, or with the other, should be clear from the contract strategy and the implications of any decision should be built into the contract plan.

Introductory comments to go in the procedures

It can be helpful if the procedures briefly touch on the legal components of a binding contract, in particular offer and acceptance. For tendering, an invitation to tender should be drafted so that it is clear that it is an invitation to treat and the procedures should stipulate this. The supplier's tender is an offer and acceptance by the procurement organisation makes the contract binding.

During negotiations, irrespective of whether they take place independently of tendering or are complementary to tendering, offer and acceptance is a continuous process which arises as the buyer and the seller make and accept or reject offer and counter-offer until they reach full agreement.

For both tendering and negotiation, the final agreement can be encapsulated in a written document which both parties sign.

It is not intended to go into any detail about contract law. Readers who are unsure should consult a legal textbook or their legal department, or may wish to consider the suitability for their organisation of products such as Knowledge Aware Limited's Contract Law INFOcharts.

Restricted tendering

The invitation to tender

The key to any tendering process is the invitation to tender. The procedures also need to make clear that it is the procurement agent who produces the invitation to tender and that other members of staff, such as the internal customer and other stakeholders, must support the requirement to do so.

The procedures need to state what should go in this document. The best approach, particularly for major procurements (especially high-risk, high-spend) is for the invitation to be divided into parts. For important tendering exercises, there are a lot of parts and all of these are described here (see Figure 11.1). However, for many invitations to tender, not all the parts will be required and the procedures should make it clear that this is the case even though it describes all of the parts.

Part 1 describes what the invitation to tender is for and gives key deadlines for delivery of the requirement. It is an introduction whose purpose is to acquaint the reader of the document with its intention.

Part 2 should deal with the process for tendering (see Figure 11.2). It consists of a number of instructions to tenderers about how they should make a tender and it should give key information about the tendering process. Approaches to tendering differ from organisation to organisation. The sealed bid system normally requires bidders to return their bids in sealed envelopes which will be opened on a certain day, sometimes at a stipulated time. All tenders have to be submitted by a given date and time which, of course, are before the opening date and time. Some organisations require that there should be no indication on the envelope which would reveal the tenderer's identify.

Tenders are often put in a special place or held by a nominated individual prior to opening and there might be rules which define how and by whom the tenders will be opened and who will attend the opening. This is discussed in more detail in the next chapter but is mentioned here because how tenders are received and opened should be indicated in this part of the invitation to tender.

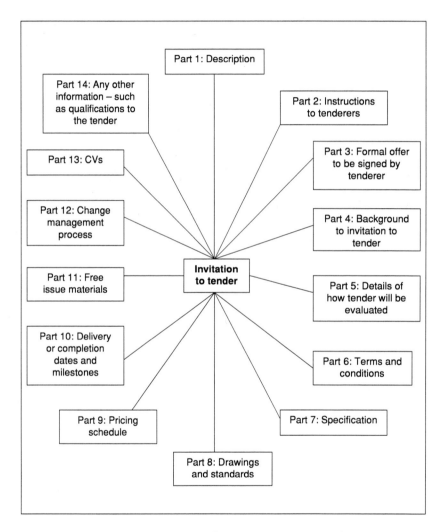

Figure 11.1 Parts of an invitation to tender.

It is also important to state that the invitation is an invitation to treat and not an offer. This avoids disputes which might arise if the supplier thought that it was responding to an offer with its acceptance, thereby creating a binding contract.

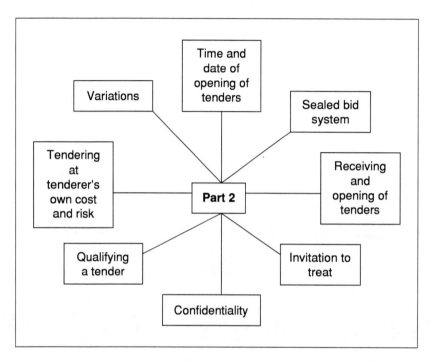

Figure 11.2 Part 2 of the invitation to tender.

Another important aspect to go into this part of the invitation to tender is how queries about the tender documents should be dealt with. The normal process is to have one person as the contact in the procurement organisation. This person will obtain the answers to any queries and then it is usual to circulate them not just to the tenderer raising the query but to all other tenderers for the sake of fairness.

The confidential nature of the bidding process should be mentioned. If this is deemed not to be an adequate safeguard, then potential tenderers should be obliged to sign a confidentiality agreement before the issue of the invitation to tender. Such tenderers should be reminded in the invitation to tender of the applicability of the confidentiality agreement.

The tenderer's right to qualify a tender, i.e. the right to say that it will not comply with a part of it, for example the payment terms and conditions or the responsibility for it to satisfy itself about a site in a construction contract, should be described. In some cases, procurement organisations will not accept any qualification and will reject any tender containing them. In other cases, qualifications are acceptable and might be the subject of further negotiation after tender receipt and analysis.

If it is intended that tendering should be entirely at the cost and risk of the tenderer, this should be stipulated and there should also be a statement in this part about how the contract will be awarded, whether by simple acceptance of the tender or by signature of a formal contract document.

Part 2 should also mention whether variations are acceptable or not. A variation is made when the bidder offers an alternative to the specified requirement. This can be very simple – a different colour or size, perhaps – or it can be an entirely different technical solution to meet the need. (*Note*: a qualification is when the tenderer wants to have different terms to those in the invitation to tender.)

It is normal for the supplier to be required to submit any qualifications or variations on pages clearly headed as being used for this purpose. This is to avoid confusion during analysis and Part 2 should make this stipulation clear.

Part 3 should be a formal offer to supply the requirement at the prices stipulated in Part 9 and on the terms and conditions specified in the invitation to tender. It should be signed by the tenderer before returning the tender. It should contain a statement about the validity period for the tender.

Part 4 of an invitation to tender might give background information such as why the requirement is needed, access to sites, etc.

Part 5 might advise how the tender will be evaluated by the procurement organisation. This is a controversial aspect and some procurement professionals would not agree that this information should be given, although in the public sector and the utilities sectors, it is a legal requirement in many countries. The advantage is that it provides a level playing field for all tenderers and it helps to prevent any fraudulent manipulation of the evaluation criteria by members of the procurement organisation's staff. It does this by making it clear that the same criteria and the same evaluation process will be applied to all. A possible disadvantage is that an unscrupulous supplier with little or no ability to meet the requirement can structure the bid so as to win the contract. However, the purpose of pre-qualification and qualification is to weed out such suppliers.

Part 6 should give the terms and conditions. There are several books about terms and conditions and many standard formats for them, so it is not intended to discuss this topic in any detail. However, to make sure that all terms and conditions are covered when bespoke terms and conditions are to be produced, the procedures should list the headings of all of the terms and conditions.

Part 7 should contain the specification.

Part 8 should contain any drawings or standards.

Part 9 should give a pricing schedule (this could be a bill of quantities) for the supplier to complete. When designing the pricing schedule, it should be remembered that it may serve two purposes, one of which is to price the eventual contract and the other is for the purposes of evaluation of the tender. If there is any conflict between these purposes, the schedule in the invitation to tender should facilitate tender evaluation and a specimen of what will appear in the contract as a pricing schedule can be included as a separate document in the invitation.

Part 10 should give the delivery or completion date for the requirement and any critical milestones which are to be met.

Part 11 should list any free issue materials.

Part 12 should describe the process for managing any changes to be made during the contract.

Part 13 is a section which requests the supplier to supply information such as the CVs of key staff.

Part 14 allows the tenderer to supply any other information which it feels might be relevant to its bid.

This seems like a lot of material. It is stressed again that not all tendering processes will require all of this material and the procurement agent needs to adapt to meet the situation. Procedures should list all of what is required for a major procurement and then make it clear that the procurement agent has the right (and should have the training and the ability) to make the necessary choices about what goes in and what is left out of an invitation to tender.

The covering letter

Invitations to tender are normally accompanied by a covering letter. The procedures should say what should be covered in such a letter, for example the dates when tenders are to be returned, the address to which they should be sent and the importance of complying with the tender instructions in Part 2 of the invitation to tender.

The main purpose of this letter is to stress important points about the tendering process and it might repeat some of the statements contained in Part 2 in order to emphasise them.

Issuing the tender

Once the invitation to tender has been drafted, the procedures should require that the necessary approvals to issue it should be obtained. The contract plan should have included this as a step in the process of issuing the invitation and it should also specify who should give the approval.

The procedures should require the procurement agent to issue the invitation to all tenderers at the same time and to give them sufficient time in which to bid. Many procurement organisations will spend a lot of time producing the invitation and then a lot more time on evaluation of the bids but allow tenderers little time to make the bid. However, the bidding is as important as any other stage in the process and it is prudent to allow bidders a sufficiently long period to tender properly.

Procedures for activities during the tendering period

The procedures should also stipulate who will act as the main contact for queries and clarifications which potential tenderers might wish to raise. Usually, this should be the procurement agent who should be required to obtain the answer to the query and circulate it to all bidders even if no other bidders have raised the matter as an issue. Queries should be obtained in writing and answers to them should be circulated in writing. The procedures should require all members of staff who are approached by the procurement agent about a query to supply answers in a timely manner.

Direct contact between internal customers or others in other parts of the organisation about the invitation to tender should be prohibited by the procedures both during and after the tender period until the contract is placed unless the members of staff concerned are part of a post-tender negotiation team. If the tenderer's query is not understood, then the matter should be raised with the tenderer by the procurement agent acting in his/her role of sole contact. The objective should, of course, be to issue an invitation which is sufficiently complete and clear that no queries are needed.

The procedures should deal with the important issue of extending the time for tendering if the queries which have been raised by tenderers make this necessary or if sufficient tenderers make it clear that insufficient time has been originally allowed for them to tender. Another possible reason for an extension is that the procurement organisation itself has issued a change to the invitation to tender and tenderers need more time to cope. In centralised and centralised/decentralised organisation structures, the authority to extend could be given by the head of procurement. In decentralised structures, a person should be nominated for this activity. In any event, it should not be a decision left to the procurement agent or the internal customer. Extending the tendering period can have implications for the procurement organisation if it is working to a tight schedule and it can also be unfair to those tenderers which might have expended a lot of effort and money to tender on time. The reason for the extension is crucial and it should, in most cases, be based on fairness to the tenderers.

Receiving the tenders

In Part 2 of the invitation to tender, the way in which tenders should be received, stored and opened should have been made clear to the potential tenderers. The procedures should describe these processes for the benefit of the procurement organisation's staff. They should make it clear:

- whether a sealed bidding process is to be used or not;

- how tenders will be referenced to ensure that the tenders are actually opened on the date specified for opening and not on some other date. Usually, this is done by requiring the envelopes containing tenders to be referenced with both a tender reference number and the date when they are to be opened. Some procurement organisations provide labels for this purpose;

- who may receive tenders;

- where they will be held.

The question of who may receive the tenders is much more important than generally recognised. Tenders are sometimes delivered by hand and left with security staff or reception staff who have no knowledge of the invitation to tender. It is not unknown for such tenders never to arrive in time to be opened, even though they have been delivered in good time. Similarly, a postroom needs to be adequately briefed about the arrival of tenders and what they should do with them.

Arrival of tenders by e-mail and fax are not recommended although sometimes permitted on the grounds of urgency. The reason for not generally permitting this method of sending tenders is that they may be read by a recipient and the information disclosed to other bidders which have not yet submitted a bid. Exceptions to the rule on the grounds of urgency need to be thought through carefully. Permission to receive bids in this way should be granted by the head of procurement in a centralised or centralised/decentralised organisation or by a designated individual in a wholly decentralised one.

Shortly before the due date for receipt of tenders, some organisations check to see how many tenders have been received. If this is so few that it indicates that there will be inadequate competition, some organisations permit the head of procurement to issue a reminder to all those invited to tender. Some organisations prefer not to do this. In either event, the procedures should deal with the matter, either permitting it and stipulating the conditions under which it is permitted or forbidding it.

Opening the tenders

Some organisations have very formal systems for opening tenders. There may be a designated body, sometimes called a tender board, which is authorised to open the tenders. The membership of the tender board may be fixed or it might be frequently changed. In other organisations, tenders are opened by a designated individual, such as the head of procurement.

In some organisations, tenders are opened in front of witnesses, which might include the bidders.

Another point of difference is how opened tenders are recorded. In some organisations, no records are kept; the tenders are opened and passed to the procurement agent or some other person such as the internal customer for evaluation. In others, there is an extensive recording process which might include noting down prices, amendments (such as crossings out or alterations) to the tenders, discrepancies (such as inaccurate arithmetic, numbers written in figures being different to numbers written in words when they should be the same) and so on.

The objective of the more rigorous processes is to avoid fraud by ensuring total transparency. The objective of the relaxed approach is to minimise bureaucracy and speed up the process.

Some organisations, usually those in the public sector, are legally obliged to adopt more rigorous processes and organisations which adopt relaxed processes need to be sure that they do not cross the fine line between relaxed and lax.

For safety's sake, and, in the case of private sector organisations, for the sake of the shareholders, procurement organisations should have tender opening processes which avoid fraud, collusion or corruption.

The procedures should specify who will open tenders. These need to be trustworthy individuals and it is wise to have more than one person engaged in the opening process and to change at least some of them at frequent intervals. Similarly, the content of tenders needs to be recorded in some way. However, it is almost impossible to do this adequately if the tender is a document of several hundred pages (or even tens of pages) without scrutinising the whole document. A possibility is to have each tender document copied (which can also be a laborious and expensive job if the document is very long) and then to keep the originals in a safe place. It is good practice to use copies of the original as working documents and to keep the original safe and *unmarked* in case of disputes, when reference can be made to the pristine original.

If it is desired to maintain a record, a note of the price and the name of the tenderer should be sufficient in most cases. It is also good practice to check for alterations and for the openers to initial these.

The procedures need to make it clear what practice is being adopted.

Two-envelope approach

The two-envelope approach is a variant of the normal tendering procedure (see Figure 11.3). Potential tenderers might be asked to supply the technical and commercial components of their bids separately. The technical component will be whatever a tenderer is proposing to meet the requirement. Separately means that the technical component and the commercial components are supplied in separate, sealed envelopes each bearing the tender reference and date. Usually, these two envelopes are put inside a third envelope which will also bear the tender reference and date.

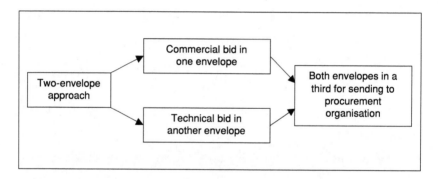

Figure 11.3 The two-envelope approach.

If this approach is required, the procedures should require a full description of the process in the invitation to tender. The procedures should also require that the contract strategy and contract plan take full account of the approach.

The procedures should also say who will evaluate the two components and the order in which they should be evaluated or who should stipulate the order in which they will be evaluated. Often, the technical component is evaluated first and the commercial component of any tenderer's bid will only be evaluated if the technical component is satisfactory.

Tenderer changing a tender

Legally, a tenderer may make and change or withdraw its tender at any time up to acceptance. Procurement organisations can stipulate that changes to a bid are not acceptable and require a validity period to the bid. The validity period prevents withdrawal of the bid: in effect the tenderer promises to keep the bid open for the validity period, which should be sufficiently long to permit the procurement organisation to receive, open and evaluate tenders, negotiate and place a contract.

Late tender

The usual rule is that late tenders will not be considered and will be returned to the tenderer unopened. The procedures should make this rule clear and a statement to this effect should also be included in Part 2 of the invitation to tender.

The procedures should say how the late tender is to be returned, usually with a brief note saying that it was late.

Sometimes, if the postmark indicates that the tender should have arrived on time, then some procurement organisations treat the late tender as having actually arrived on time. This is not recommended as it really is for the tenderer to get the tender delivered on time – the uncertainties of the mail are usually well known and other methods of delivery do exist.

Mistake in the tender

Procedures should specify what should happen if there is an obvious mistake in the tender or if the tender is abnormally low. The usual approach is to write and ask the tenderer to confirm that the error is what was intended but not to specifically say that there is suspicion that there is an error. This should be sufficient to alert the tenderer that there is some dubiety about what has been offered in the tender without actually saying so.

If the tenderer confirms what has been offered, the tender evaluation should be conducted on the basis of the confirmation.

However, a little common sense is needed. If the tenderer has committed a mistake but has not been sufficiently acute to realise this when receiving the query, then a contract placed on this basis is unlikely to be easy to manage. Eventually, during the contract period, the tenderer (now the supplier) will realise the mistake and could seek to ameliorate the situation, for example by reducing the level of service or the quality or by raising claims and so on. Some of these measures might be legitimate but they will not be conducive to a good working relationship. Procurement organisations should ask themselves whether they really want to run the risk, especially if the gain made by accepting the supplier's offer is low.

Open tendering

Open tendering is used mainly in the public sector. The process is illustrated in Figure 11.4.

An invitation to tender is produced in the same way as for restricted tendering. The difference between the two processes is that the potential tenderers are selected using pre-qualification and, possibly, qualification for the restricted process. In the open process, an advertisement is placed usually in local papers, trade magazines and the like. The advertisement gives details of the requirement and invites those interested in tendering to apply for the invitation to tender. Invitations are issued to all applicants.

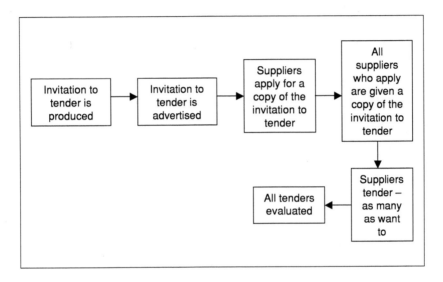

Figure 11.4 Open tendering.

Proponents of this form of tendering claim that it should lead to better prices as there is more competition and that it is fairer as it gives all possible tenderers an opportunity to bid. It is also sometimes argued that open tendering helps to prevent fraud or corruption by making it difficult for a corrupt person in the procurement organisation to manipulate bidders lists.

The contrary arguments are that well conducted pre-qualification should ensure that competition is stimulated between those best able to offer good prices or low whole-life costs. Pre-qualification should also be sufficiently open to permit any supplier to be considered and manipulation of bidders lists is avoided by having a rigorous qualification process. The open process does not prevent corrupt manipulation at some other part of the process, such as during tender evaluation.

The prime disadvantage of open tendering is that it can mean a lot of tenders, some, possibly many, of which might not be worth evaluating as they are technically or commercially unsatisfactory. It can mean a lot of work and not just for the procurement organisation but also for all the bidders who are rejected. The overall cost is higher to the economy as a whole although this is borne by the individual bidders and the procurement organisation.

The procedures need to address how the advertisements should be drafted and in what media they should be placed. The procedures should stipulate a cut-off date for applications for the invitation to tender documents and say how applications should be made.

The process for producing an invitation to tender is the same as has been described under the restricted tendering process. The procedures should make this clear.

Single tendering and sole tendering

The distinction between these two processes has been discussed above.

Fundamentally, the process for issuing an invitation to tender in either of these cases is no different to issuing an invitation to tender in a situation where competition exists.

The procedures should concern themselves with ensuring that the circumstance is a single source or sole source situation. If it is a single source situation, the procedures should require that the invitation to tender is issued in such a way that the tenderer believes that tendering is taking place in competitive circumstances. This is not always possible but it can lead to better offers.

Negotiation

There are many books and courses which deal with negotiation techniques. It is intended to limit the discussion here to what should appear in procurement procedures.

There are three occasions when negotiation might be necessary:

- in order to let a contract without using tendering;

- in order to improve offers already made by tenderers;

- in order to settle post-contractual claims made by suppliers or made by the procurement organisation.

The procedures should require negotiation to improve offers already made by tenderers to be conducted with not less than three tenderers wherever possible so that competition is maintained.

In general, the procedures should require officers conducting negotiations:

- to be not less than two, one of whom should take notes. The two could consist of the procurement agent and the internal customer;

- to circulate the notes of the negotiation meeting to the supplier involved and obtain the supplier's agreement that they are an accurate record of what took place;

- to have established criteria for evaluating negotiated offers. This will often mean deciding what is the minimum acceptable offer and what is the most desirable. Negotiations are conducted to achieve the most desirable with the minimum as a fallback position;

- to have established that they have the authority to negotiate. The procedures will have to say who can confer that authority;

- to not hold themselves out as having the authority to commit the procurement organisation during the negotiation. It is advisable for the officers to make this clear at the onset of the negotiations or even in writing before they begin;

- to clear any negotiation strategy or ploys before the negotiation with an appropriately designated person within the procurement organisation;

- to not engage in any practices which are untruthful or mislead the supplier.

The procedures should also say what is to be the process for selecting the officers and how the outcome of any negotiation is to be approved within the organisation.

CHAPTER 12

Evaluation, letting the contract, contract management and data management

How tenders are to be evaluated will depend on the relationship between risk and spend. For convenience, the model is repeated in Figure 12.1.

Evaluation

Procurements falling into Box 1

Procurements falling into Box 1 are of great importance to the procurement organisation. It is likely that the emphasis will be on value. This has been discussed previously and it is a blend of various characteristics such as conformance to specification, quality,

---

delivery, internal customer satisfaction and so on, all of which are expressed as a function of whole-life cost.

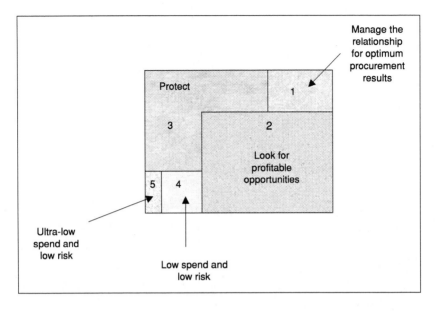

Figure 12.1 Risk–spend matrix.

The first step in any evaluation is to identify the components of value for any particular procurement. A weighting needs to be determined for each of these components as they might not all have identical importance. Each of the components is then scored out of some suitable number, say 100, and the weighting applied to obtain the weighted score for that component. These should be added to obtain the total weighted score.

As with pre-qualification, it is quite possible that there are some components which are essential and a failure of a tenderer to achieve a high score on these would disqualify the tender.

The assignment of weightings and the scoring should be as rational as possible but the appraisal is nevertheless subjective. To counter this, teams may be used to score. Team members score individually and then meet to share and challenge each other's results and opinions. The objective is to arrive at a final score which is as rational as possible.

The next step is to calculate the whole-life cost. Dividing the whole-life cost by the total weighted score will give a value of £ per unit score point. If this calculation is done for all tenders, then the lowest of these provides the best value.

The calculation of whole-life cost is a commercial matter which requires a knowledge of discounted cash flow techniques. Readers not familiar with this technique should consult financial textbooks or take advice from their organisation's finance department.

Procurements falling into Box 2

There is no reason why a similar process should not be applied to Box 2. However, procurements falling into this box are considered to be possible sources of profit for the procurement organisation as there is little risk to the organisation and aggressive tendering and/or negotiation can be used to obtain the lowest prices or whole-life cost.

This means that the value tends towards being the lowest price or whole-life cost. This approach assumes that all the other value components are unimportant or they are the same for all bids and so they can be disregarded. However, low risk does not necessarily mean that the value can be disregarded in this way and procurement organisations need to think carefully before they do.

Procurements falling into Box 3

The main concern here is to protect the organisation. Security of supply has to be a component of value. There needs to be a high weighting given to this and there also needs to be a high threshold score for security which suppliers should meet if they are to be considered for a contract.

In practice, obtaining supplies might be so important that security of supply is the only factor considered and cost and other value factors are almost disregarded.

Procurements falling into Boxes 4 and 5

In almost all cases, price will be the major consideration for procurements falling into Box 4 and this will certainly be true of procurements in Box 5 (see Figure 12.2).

Of course, there are occasions when delivery or quality or some other component of value will be very important even for procurements which fall into these boxes. However, the method of evaluation is not likely to be as rigorous as that discussed above. It is quite likely to be left to the gut feel of the procurement agent or the internal customer.

What the procedures should say about evaluation

It is not possible for procedures to be too prescriptive about how tenders or the outcomes of negotiations should be evaluated. The most suitable method and the evaluation criteria for any particular procurement should be described in the contract strategy.

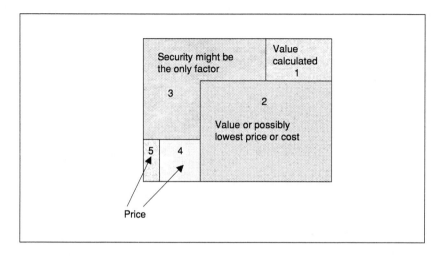

Figure 12.2 Main considerations for Boxes 4 and 5.

The procedures should outline the steps in the evaluation of value (see Figure 12.3) but leave it to the procurement agent and the internal customer to decide how the evaluation should be conducted in particular cases.

For complex procurements, evaluation might need to be conducted by a team consisting of personnel from procurement, the internal customer and other stakeholders. The procedures should indicate how the teams should be selected.

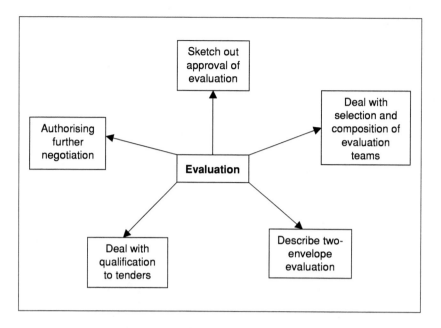

Figure 12.3 Steps in the evaluation of value.

They should also describe how a two-envelope evaluation will be conducted. This is normally done by having an evaluation of the technical proposal for the requirement and an independent commercial evaluation. Often, these two evaluations are conducted by separate teams. The technical evaluation should be conducted using the scoring and weighting process and solutions should be listed in order of preference. The commercial evaluation is likely to be an evaluation of whole-life cost. The method of ranking the tenders has been described above.

Of particular importance is the need to review any qualifications to the tender. A decision has to be made about their acceptability.

This needs to be done after consultation with the appropriate experts, such as the legal and finance departments.

If, after evaluation, the evaluators are of the opinion that the deals on offer could be improved by negotiation, the procedures should require that they approach the head of procurement in centralised or centralised/decentralised organisations or some suitably designated person in totally decentralised organisations for authority to conduct further negotiations. If approval is granted, then the procedures should require that negotiations are conducted as described in Chapter 11.

Letting the contract

Once the evaluation has been completed, the procedures should require that it is submitted for approval for letting. The procedures should specify who will approve the letting of contracts and the spend values which they are authorised to sign off (see Chapter 7).

If the person who is authorised to approve the letting of the contract does not believe that the proposed contract is satisfactory, he or she may recommend that further negotiations be conducted with the tenderers.

When a satisfactory deal has been reached, the procedures should offer a choice of ways of letting the contract. If the tenders have not been subsequently modified by negotiation and there were no significant qualifications to the invitation to tender, then there is no reason why they could not simply be accepted by letter from the procurement organisation to the successful tenderer. If, on the other hand, the original bids have been modified or if the bids have been changed as a result of post-tender negotiation or if the offers have been arrived at purely through a process of negotiation, then it is usual to draft a contract.

This contract document should be sent to the successful tenderer for verification that it does correspond exactly with what has been agreed. This should be a formality if the notes of any negotiation have been circulated to and agreed by the tenderer. It is then customary for two copies of the document to be signed by the representative of the procurement organisation, witnessed (if required) and dated and for both to be sent to the tenderer with the request that one is signed, witnessed and dated and returned to the procurement organisation. Another approach is for the representatives of the tenderer to be invited to the procurement organisation where both parties sign the agreement and it is witnessed and dated.

The procedures should require the procurement agent to advise unsuccessful tenderers only after a contract is in place. The procurement agent should produce a list of information which will be imparted to unsuccessful tenderers in order to explain the reason for their failure to win the contract. The information should be discussed and agreed with the internal customer, the head of legal services and other appropriate members of staff (for example the finance department if the reason for rejection of a bid was failure to agree or offer suitable payment terms). The brief should be approved by the head of procurement or by a suitable person in decentralised organisations.

The procedures should require the information to be imparted verbally either on the telephone or in a meeting and they should require that the procurement agent does not depart from the information which has been agreed. A note of any comments made by unsuccessful tenderers and any responses to them should be retained.

Contract management

The degree of contract management depends on the type of contract. For procurements in Boxes 4 and 5 in Figure 12.1 above, contract management is likely to be no more than progressing receipt of goods in an undamaged state. For services, it will simply be ensuring the services are delivered on time and to an acceptable quality. The same might be true of Box 3 and some procurements in Box 2. However, for some procurements in these boxes and most probably for all procurements in Box 1, contract management is likely to be a more extensive exercise, particularly if the procurement is of the nature of a project involving the delivery of goods and/or services over a period of time.

Contract management tends to be *specific to a procurement*. The procedures can only address matters of principle by highlighting where poor contract management can occur and by requiring steps to be taken to ensure that good contract management takes place. What follows here is a discussion of what should appear in such procedures. It is of course for the parties involved in the procurement, most notably the procurement agent as part of his or her leading role in the process, to adapt the principles to the particular circumstance.

It can be helpful for the procedures to list those causes of poor contract management which arise before the contract is let:

- poor risk assessment;

- poorly drafted specifications which require changes after the contract has been let;

- poor supplier selection – pre-qualification and qualification should be designed to avoid this;

- poor contract drafting resulting in unclear or omitted contract terms;

- unclear roles – failure to specify who does what;

- poor relationships.

The objective of this list is to emphasise the importance of preparation *before letting the contract.*

Contract management involves a number of departments in a variety of roles. The procedures should indicate what these are. Table 12.1 is illustrative.

Table 12.1 draws attention to the fact that contract management is a cross-departmental activity. The procedures should require that the contract management responsibilities of individuals are clearly defined at the contract strategy stage and that all individuals know what is expected of them.

Poor relationships are also a cause of poor contract management. These can be internal, i.e. one person with another within the procurement organisation, but more usually they arise between persons in the procurement organisation and the supplier. Likely reasons for poor relationships are a clash of personalities, sharp practice and very differing objectives.

Table 12.1 Roles and responsibilities in contract management

Role	Responsibility
Procurement	Commercial decision-making
	Negotiations
	Claims management
	Contract interpretation
	Liaison with legal department
	Etc.
Internal customers	Liaison with supplier about delivery, receipt of goods/services
	Decisions about quality and acceptability of goods/services
	Authorisation of any technical changes
Legal department	Provide specialist advice
	Etc.
Finance department	Provide specialist advice
	Clear invoices
	Manage budgets
	Etc.

It helps if the procedures list these reasons to highlight their existence and to encourage participants in the contract management process to guard against them.

An essential feature of all contract management is measurement of supplier performance. Again, this should have been addressed at the contract strategy stage and appropriate mechanisms for measuring performance built into the contract. The procedures should insist on the application of a sound supplier performance measurement process.

Milestones are essential for monitoring a supplier's performance and these should have been included in the contract.

Poorly managed change after the letting of a contract is a major source of poor contract management. For preference change should be avoided and, if there has been a rigorous procurement process, change should not be a frequent occurrence. However, change cannot always be avoided and the procedures should cater for this situation by requiring that a good change management process is included in the contract. Again, this is something which needs to be thought out at the contract strategy stage. The question is not just what the supplier has to do to manage change but also what the procurement organisation should do. Changes should be fully costed and documented before there is agreement to undertake them. There should be properly agreed milestones to monitor progress in implementing the change.

Last but not least, the procedures should require that costs are monitored during the contract as a key part of good contract management.

Data management

All procurement work generates a significant amount of records. Increasingly these are now electronic records.

The procedures need to stipulate what records should be held. The following is a list of possible documents which should be retained:

- the contract strategy and the contract plan;

- pre-qualification questionnaires and criteria;

- lists of suppliers which were pre-qualified, their pre-qualification scores and any correspondence;

- information concerning supplier qualification;

- information about the invitation to tender – its development and use;

- information about tender evaluation, contract approval, letting the contract;

- a copy of the contract;

- information about contract management: details of meetings, variations, concessions, correspondence, timesheets, goods received notes, invoices, etc.;

- market information;

- price/cost trend information for commodities and statistics about market rates.

With both paper and electronic systems, these documents could be held by a variety of people in a variety of locations. The procedures should address the question of traceability by requiring a record to be kept of where the documents are and, possibly, by insisting on there being a master copy at a single location.

It will be necessary to stipulate who should be responsible for the safekeeping of the documents – usually this should be the procurement agent. Other members of staff should be required to assist the procurement agent by declaring what documents they possess and making them available as necessary.

The procedures should also mention the legal requirement to retain contractual documents for six years.

CHAPTER 13

Purchasing cards

Use of cards

The original use of purchasing cards was to handle the low-risk, low-spend requirements of an organisation. These are the types of spend which fall into the bottom left-hand box of the risk–spend matrix. In some organisations, this type of spend might be as much as 70 per cent of all procurement transactions.

However, some organisations now use purchasing cards for other purposes, such as paying for requirements which fall into the bottom right-hand box (low risk/high spend) or for requirements which are e-procured either through an intranet or a marketplace or directly from other organisations' websites.

Main advantages

The main advantage of purchasing cards (see Figure 13.1) is that they reduce the number of invoices and simplify payment, often reducing the payment of many invoices down to the payment of a single invoice from the card issuer. Using purchasing cards can eliminate the need for requisitions and for orders depending on the extent to which these have been previously used for low-risk/low-spend procurement. Calculations of the cost of processing a procurement transaction lead to various results depending on what is included in the calculation. Figures of approximately £60, excluding accounts payable (a 2003 study conducted by Accenture, 'Procurement to Payment Processes and the Role of Procurement Cards' gave a figure of US$97) are often quoted. Streamlining the process has the potential to generate significant savings in process costs.

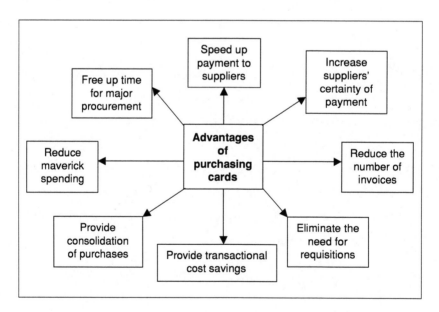

Figure 13.1 Advantages of purchasing cards.

Other advantages claimed are those normally associated with good procurement, such as consolidation of purchases which might lead to lower prices, less maverick purchasing which gives suppliers offering lower prices more confidence that the price reductions will be justified by increased business, and more time for procurement practitioners to concentrate on high-value and/or high-risk purchases.

The advantages for the supplier are the speed and certainty of payment. Card issuers pay suppliers promptly.

How cards work

From a user's point of view, the cards all work similarly although their features are not identical. The differences are discussed later in this chapter.

Basically, the purchaser contacts a supplier which is prepared to accept payment by means of a purchasing card. The purchaser gives the supplier the card number in exchange for the goods or services to be bought. This might mean giving the card physically to the supplier for the supplier to swipe through a point-of-sale machine or simply giving the card number for the supplier to input electronically via a keyboard. Eighty per cent of purchasing card transactions are typically carried out over the telephone.

If the card is a MasterCard or VISA card, an electronic signal is sent to the card issuer, which is usually a bank, via the card association, i.e. via MasterCard or VISA. The card issuer, i.e. the bank, pays the supplier within 2–4 days following the transaction. If the card is an American Express (Amex) card, an electronic signal is sent to American Express which makes payment within five banking days. Amex thus effectively combines the roles of card issuer and card provider.

The amount paid is usually the price of the goods or services which have been supplied minus the agreed Merchant Service Charge (typically 2–2.5 per cent of the purchase price). The card issuer or Amex invoices the purchaser once a month for all the purchases made in that month and may have a direct debit arrangement for payment. There is usually a period of grace before the direct debit is activated in order to give the purchaser a chance to query any items on the bill.

Contractual relationships

These are quite complex. There is a contractual relationship between the procurement organisation and the supplier. The procurement organisation's terms and conditions should make it clear that payment for the goods and services purchased by that organisation will be made by purchasing card and that the money will come from the card issuer.

There is also a contractual relationship between the purchasing card issuer and the procurement organisation which governs the issue and use of the cards. In return for the card issuer paying the supplier, the procurement organisation agrees to pay the card issuer within an agreed period from the date of the card issuer's invoice. Payment may be made by direct debit.

There is also a contractual relationship between the card issuer and the supplier which will guarantee payment by the card issuer subject to the satisfaction of the procurement organisation with the goods and/or services which have been bought.

VAT

For invoices above £5,000, the Customs & Excise are prepared to permit a procurement organisation to reclaim any VAT paid when purchasing using a card provided a VAT report from the card issuer shows line item detail. This is basically a statement of each individual purchase showing the name of the supplier, the date of transmission by the supplier to the card issuer of the information about the transaction and the supplier's VAT number. The VAT rate and the VAT paid has to be recorded against each line item. This concession by the Customs & Excise means that there is no need to obtain an individual VAT invoice from each supplier for each purchase made using a purchasing card.

Suppliers must not send the procurement organisation an invoice requiring payment as this might create confusion by establishing more than one source of evidence of the VAT paid for the same transaction. Of course, the procurement organisation would not want an invoice from the supplier because the procurement organisation pays the card issuer. Consequently, no invoice is required from the supplier and the only invoice which the procurement organisation wants to see is the one from the card issuer. If, for some reason, the supplier wishes to send a pro-forma invoice to the procurement organisation, it must bear the words to the effect that the document is for information only and does not provide evidence of VAT paid.

Customs & Excise will also permit VAT to be reclaimed on a summary invoice, i.e. an invoice not showing line item detail, provided the total amount of the invoice is less than £5,000 excluding VAT. The summary invoice must contain the following information:

- value of the supply;

- VAT amount charged;

- VAT note;

- time of supply;

- description of the goods or service supplied;

- supplier's name, address and VAT number;

- procurement organisation's name and address.

If, using the summary invoice approach, a single transaction exceeds £5,000, it is necessary to obtain a full, normal VAT invoice from the supplier in addition to the summary invoice from the card issuer.

If a purchasing card is used at a retail establishment, the level of information is not sufficient for either of the above processes to apply and a VAT receipt must be obtained from the retailer in the same way that a receipt is necessary for petty cash transactions.

Card issuers

There are several card issuers and at least fifty cards are available, although many of these are restricted to the purchase of a single category of goods or services, such as fuel for vehicles, travel or the goods/services sold by the card issuer.

Purchasing cards for the purchase of a range of goods and services are normally serviced by American Express (Amex), VISA and MasterCard. American Express issues its own cards and acts as both the card issuer and the card service provider. VISA and MasterCard do not issue cards themselves. Their cards are issued by a number of banks in the UK and the service provided is pretty much the same for each card of this type.

In this chapter, the expression 'card issuer' has been used to describe the organisation which issues the card to the procurement organisation. In the case of MasterCard and VISA this is usually a bank. The normal expression used for banks issuing cards is 'acquirer'. This is because the bank acquires suppliers, i.e. it persuades the suppliers to accept the cards as a means of payment. Within a bank the card issuing role and the supplier acquirer role can be undertaken by different departments. For VISA and MasterCard, it is perfectly possible to use a card issued by one bank with a supplier acquired by another. Each type of card can only be used with suppliers which accept that type of card, e.g. a MasterCard card can only be used with suppliers that accept MasterCard, an Amex card can only be used with suppliers which accept Amex and so on.

As has been mentioned above, for its card, Amex acts as card issuer, supplier acquirer and card service provider.

Both VISA and MasterCard cards can be used in any of the outlets normally prepared to accept credit card facilities from these companies. This means that all retail outlets and businesses such as builders' merchants will be prepared to accept the business purchasing card. Although VISA and MasterCard issuers will, acting in their supplier acquirer role, add new suppliers at the request of the procurement organisation, it is normally considered that there are sufficient outlets already available to meet the needs of most procurement organisations.

Amex does not have so many retail etc. outlets accepting its card. Amex will therefore involve themselves much more in developing a supplier network for a procurement organisation. This can involve checks being conducted by Amex to assure itself that the supplier is satisfactory.

Both Amex and the card issuing banks often do not issue a card. They simply issue a 'card' number (or numbers) to a procurement organisation and the organisation quotes the number to the supplier. In the rest of this chapter, reference is made to the card. This should be taken to mean the 'card' number in those cases where Amex or the card issuing banks do not actually issue a card.

Amex also gives line item detail on its invoices as a matter of course. This is important for VAT recovery (see above).

One card or many?

The choice is illustrated in Figure 13.2.

One card number per procurement organisation

A procurement organisation may have a single card account number. The card number could be distributed around the organisation to various individuals in various departments and used by them to make their purchases. As there would be only one number, there would be a single invoice from the card issuer. However, the purchases on the invoice could be made by a number of different individuals and this makes it difficult to check the invoice to be sure that goods/services have been received prior to payment or to ensure that there has been no abuse of the card, for example its being used for private purchases. It will also be difficult to charge back to cost centres the costs which they have incurred by using the card. This is because it is difficult to capture cost centre information at the point of sale.

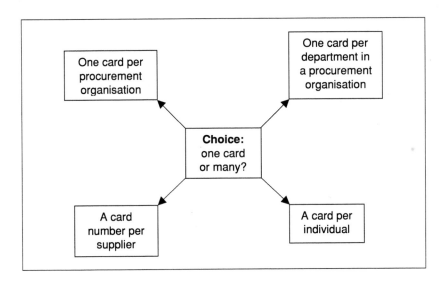

Figure 13.2 One card or many?

An alternative approach, used by some companies, is to have a single person in the company authorised to use the purchasing card on behalf of the company. This means that anybody wishing to buy something must contact that person for the card to be used.

The person authorised to use the purchasing card will contact the supplier and agree that payment should be made by purchasing card. This obviously has advantages in that it controls the use of the card; however, it does not reduce the administration as much as other ways of using the card. The invoice again comes from the card issuer.

One card number per department in a procurement organisation

An option is for the organisation to have a number of different card account numbers and to assign one number to each department in the organisation. A specific individual in each department is responsible for this number and he or she does all the purchasing for that department. This will mean a single monthly invoice per card number for each department. This increases the number of invoices compared to having a single card number per procurement organisation, although the number of invoices will still be much less than the number handled in pre-card times. This approach gives some control over the purchasing process by ensuring that a specified individual in a department is responsible for the purchasing done on that card. The individual can be asked to certify the invoice for that department before payment is due. This gives an opportunity to query payments which do not seem to be genuine. However, having only a single individual can be restrictive, particularly if that individual is not available owing to holidays, sickness or a workload involving lots of meetings.

It is possible to overcome this difficulty by having a separate number for each department and by issuing that number to many individuals in the department. This means that there will be one invoice for the department but that invoice will cover the purchases of several people. This approach provides flexibility by ensuring that there is always somebody available who knows the card number but it can still be difficult to know who spent what on what unless some record is kept.

A card number per individual

A further possibility is to issue a card to any individual who needs one. This means an invoice per card, which could mean more invoices than any other approach but there is direct traceability of the spend to the individual.

A card number per supplier

Finally, it is possible to have an account number for a supplier, so that each supplier could have a different account number to any other supplier. This has attractions if the procurement is to be restricted to suppliers with which a lot of business is to be done and normally there should be framework agreements with these suppliers. The card cannot be used for any purchases of items not covered by the framework agreement; in other words, it prevents ad hoc purchasing. Such purchasing will have to be done in some other way and this will almost certainly mean low-value invoices, the very circumstances which the purchasing card is intended to avoid. Alternatively, there can be another card for ad hoc purchases. A disadvantage of a supplier card is that it is not possible to charge back costs to individual cost-centres because, as previously mentioned, cost centre information is not captured at the point of sale.

One card or many – which approach?

Each organisation must make its choice depending on its circumstances. However, there are some advantages to having more than one card number.

With one card, there will be a need for a higher spend limit than might be necessary for individual cards with different numbers. This is because the whole of the procurement organisation's purchasing card spend goes through that card, whereas in the many card scenario, each department will have its own uniquely numbered card and the spend will be attributed to that number. Any department's spend must be lower than the total for the organisation, consequently the spend limit on the individual card may be lower.

Several differently numbered cards mean that the controls can be customised to each card, i.e. it is possible to set different transaction limits, monthly limits and supplier restrictions. The main advantage is that spend is traceable and chargeable to individual cost centres. These advantages have to be offset against the fact that there will be more card issuer invoices but the total number should be significantly less than occurred before the cards were used.

Eliminating orders

Purchasing cards can eliminate the need to raise a requisition and a purchase order. This may make many orders simply verbal contracts, but even if there is some written correspondence, such as e-mails, it is unlikely that any terms and conditions will be agreed. Some organisations get over this problem by having framework agreements with selected suppliers and then restricting the use of the card to these suppliers.

Procedures required to manage purchasing cards

This chapter does not deal with the introduction of purchasing cards into an organisation. Their introduction is best managed as a project which is rolled out in discrete steps, and there are various project management techniques which may help. This chapter deals with the procedures needed to manage cards once they are in situ. Many of the matters to be discussed need to be considered during the project and even before it.

The chapter is also not intended to be a detailed source of information about purchasing cards and especially about VAT implications. Readers should not make a choice of card or decide their approach to VAT on the basis of the information contained in this chapter.

The remainder of this chapter considers the contents of procedures which a procurement organisation may need to use the cards.

Contact with the card issuer

The organisation should have some person who will act as the central contact point for the card issuer. This person should be able to deal with any contractual issues which may arise with the card issuer. The person should also be responsible for the management and control of cards after their initial issue.

The procedures should state who this person is. Normally in organisations where procurement is centralised, this will be the head of procurement or a designated officer in his or her department. In an organisation whose procurement is conducted on a centralised/decentralised basis, the contact could still be the head of procurement, especially if the same purchasing card is to be used across the organisation.

In organisations where procurement is decentralised, it will be necessary to designate a person in each decentralised unit. In the absence of any head of procurement in each unit, this could be some person in the finance department.

Irrespective of the structure of procurement in the organisation, the procedures should make it clear that all other personnel deal with the card issuing company through this designated person, although individual queries about any item of spend could be handled directly by personnel with the card issuing company.

The designated person is called the 'card manager' in the rest of this chapter. It is possible for the card manager's role to be split. In large, more complex organisations, three roles might be envisaged:

- a senior sponsor (such as the head of procurement) responsible for the governance, strategy and programme direction;

- a programme/project manager, responsible for implementing purchasing card projects;

- a programme administrator, responsible for administration and maintenance of cards and card accounts. This person will be the day-to-day operational contact both internally and with the card issuer.

Contact with the supplier

Contact with the supplier of the goods/services will normally be made only by the personnel making the purchase using the card. There are two exceptions to this rule. Firstly, it will be the head of procurement in either a centralised or centralised/decentralised structure who will establish framework agreements when these are used to facilitate the purchase. Secondly, it might very occasionally be necessary for the head of procurement or procurement staff to become involved in the event of a dispute with the supplier.

The procedures should define the information to be given to suppliers when making a purchase using the purchasing card. This information may include:

- name of the buyer;

- the card number;

- expiration date of the card;

- delivery address for the goods;

- department name and location;

- business telephone details.

Framework agreements

A major cause for concern has been that issuing purchasing cards will encourage rather than discourage maverick purchasing. Some organisations endeavour to overcome this by establishing framework agreements. A feature of these agreements is payment by purchasing card. It can, however, be restrictive if the card can only be used in association with framework agreements. The procedures need to make it clear that framework agreements should be used where they exist and that the card is not to be used to purchase goods or services from suppliers other than those which can be designated on a framework agreement unless the 'framework agreement' supplier is unable to supply.

It is possible with the Amex card to restrict the use of the card to specific suppliers. These 'Preferred Supplier Restrictions' block out non-preferred suppliers and thus prevent maverick purchasing.

Procedures for approving a card application

The procedures required for approving a card application are outlined in Figure 13.3. After the initial provision of the cards within the procurement organisation, replacement cards will need to be provided when the card issuer issues a new card or when another member of staff is to be provided with a card. In the first case, all the original cards need to be withdrawn and destroyed and new ones provided. In the second case, it will be necessary to provide the card and to ensure that the member of staff receives some training in its use.

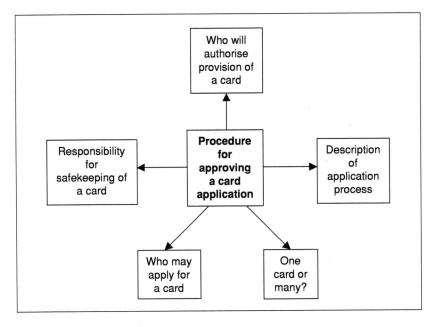

Figure 13.3 Procedures for approving a card application.

The procedures need to state who will provide cards. This is really a case of who may authorise the provision of a card as the cards themselves will normally be sent by the card issuing company directly to the user. In organisations where the procurement is centralised or centralised/decentralised, the person authorising the provision of a card should be the head of procurement acting in his or her role as card manager. In decentralised organisations, there will need to be a designated officer – the head of finance is a possible backstop.

The procedures should also state who may have a card. This has been discussed in the sections above on 'One card or many?'

There should be a statement about who may apply for a card. For example, if it is intended to only provide cards to persons of a certain level of authority in the organisation, then this should be stated so that individuals who do not meet this requirement do not apply. More junior staff should have their applications for a card endorsed by their management and the procedures should make clear which persons in the organisation may endorse such an application.

If the card is to be provided to a department, the procedures should say who in the department may apply and any necessary authorisations which must be obtained. Generally, this will be done by reference to positions or levels of authority.

The procedures should stipulate that the individual to whom the card is issued is responsible for its safe keeping and its use. Failure to look after the card and illegitimate use may be a cause for disciplinary action and the procedures should make this clear. Where the same card number is given to persons in the same department, it might be desirable to impose on the manager of that department a supervisory responsibility with respect to the use of the card. However, this should be done without any detraction from the responsibilities of the persons to whom the card number has been issued. Control is easier if each person has a uniquely numbered card.

The procedures should describe the application process. Normally, there should be a written application stating:

- the sorts of things which are likely to be bought;

- the suppliers and framework agreements to be used – this should help identify merchant codes with which the card can be programmed (see section on 'use of the card' below);

- whether there will be any ad hoc purchasing from suppliers with which no framework exists;

- the amount likely to be spent each month – this can be used to set a monthly transaction limit (see section on 'use of the card' below);

- the transaction limit required (see section on 'use of the card' below);

- the arrangements for vetting the invoice from the card issuer;

- who will use the card (this can also be used to limit the use of the card);

- how it will be kept secure;

- who authorises the application (signature, name and title).

The procedures should say to whom the application should be sent, who will approve the application and who will implement it. Approval and implementation should be the responsibility of the card manager. The procedures also need to say whether the card manager will provide the card (after receiving it him or herself from the card issuer) or whether the card will be issued directly by the card issuer. If the latter, the card manager needs to be kept informed.

The procedures should require the card holder to sign the card as soon as it has been received. The procedures should also require the card holder not to allow any other person to use the card for any purpose. Failure to do either of these might be the subject of a disciplinary offence.

Use of the card

Using electronic coding, it is possible to limit the use of a card as follows:

- restrictions to certain merchant categories (e.g. it is possible to restrict a card so that it can be used to buy building supplies but not stationery);

- restrictions on the size of a spend on any single transaction, for example if the card had a single transaction limit of £500, then it could not be used to purchase anything more than £500 in a single transaction. This is intended to prevent the card from being used to purchase expensive items without any authority;

- restrictions on the amount which may be spent in any month;

- restrictions on the supplier categories (MasterCard and VISA) or on actual suppliers (Amex) from which purchases can be made using the card.

The card issuer can code in any of the above restrictions at the request of the procurement organisation.

The procedures should make it clear that these restrictions will be applied and the extent to which they will be applied. The restrictions should be addressed in the application for a card (see the section on 'issue of cards' above).

With these restrictions, it should be difficult for the use of the card to be abused in any way. However, human ingenuity is as good at finding ways of circumnavigating safeguards as it is of inventing and establishing the safeguards in the first place. Use of the card should always conform with the application for the card.

A point for any procurement organisation to bear in mind is that the spend limits mentioned above need to be realistic. If they are set too low, card holders will not be able to use the cards when required. There will probably be a high number of rejections if they try to use the cards for amounts in excess of the limit. This has many disadvantages: it brings the cards into disrepute with the card holders, looks bad to suppliers witnessing the rejections and causes unnecessary administration.

Ordering from a supplier

If a framework agreement exists with the supplier, then the procedures should require that the agreement makes it plain that the card will used for payment and that such transactions are subject to the terms and conditions agreed in the framework agreement. In general, the procedures should require framework agreements to be put in place with all suppliers from whom frequent purchases are to be made.

If purchases are to be made on an ad hoc basis from suppliers with which there is no framework agreement, then it is possible that no terms and conditions will have been agreed in which case common law as modified by statute and interpreted by the courts will apply. It is also possible that the purchase will be on the supplier's terms and conditions of sale. However, depending on what has been agreed, it is also possible that the purchase will be on the procurement organisation's terms and conditions of purchase.

The most usual outcome is that nobody really knows which of the above three possibilities apply. For this reason and in order to manage disputes should any arise, the procedures should require the card holder to keep a record of any purchases made (called the 'purchase record sheet' in later parts of this chapter), particularly if the purchase is to be made orally, for example over the telephone.

The record should show

- an exact description of what has been ordered;

- the date when ordered;

- quantity;

- the price, VAT and agreed delivery;

- the supplier's name and the name of the person handling the order at the supplier's;

- the supplier's order confirmation number – if any;

- a note of any terms and conditions which have been agreed. This might be a reference to a framework agreement. If neither party makes reference to terms and conditions then that fact should be recorded here. It is highly likely that raising the subject of terms and conditions will delay the purchase as the other party will want to see the proposed terms and conditions. Such delays tend to negate the advantages of purchasing cards by introducing complexity. In most cases for the types of goods and services to be purchased on an ad hoc basis, the absence of terms and conditions is not likely to be a serious problem.

This purchase record sheet could be a paper or an electronic record. The order could be verbal or an e-mail, letter or fax or a normal order form. The latter tend not to help the reduction in paperwork which is the prime objective of the purchasing card.

It is useful to keep a diary of promised deliveries (the delivery diary) so that late deliveries can be identified and progressed with the supplier if necessary.

When the goods and services have been received, the purchase record sheet and the delivery diary should be noted. This can facilitate reconciliation of the invoices from the card issuer.

Loss of a card and replacement

The procedures need to address what steps must be taken if a card is lost or stolen. Normally, the card holder should be empowered to contact the card issuer immediately so that blocks on the use of the card can be put in place immediately. The card manager should be notified preferably at the same time and he or she should check that the card issuer has cancelled the card and issued another one.

Changes to the card

From time to time, card users may wish to increase the monthly transaction limit or extend the range of suppliers with which they may trade using the card.

The procedures need to make it clear how this may be done. Application should be made in writing to the card manager and authorised by the same person as authorised the original application for a card. The card manager should consider the application and approve or reject it. Rejection will naturally require discussion with the originator of the application and with the person who authorised it.

If approved, the matter then needs to be taken up with the card issuer by the card manager.

Replacing cards

From time to time, card issuers replace cards. The objective is partly preventative maintenance: if real cards are being used, the magnetic strip degrades over time. The replacement may also be for security purposes.

It should be the responsibility of the card manager to ensure that the card issuer has a full, up-to-date list of all card holders. It follows that the procedures should require the card manager to administer this list and to check its accuracy from time to time. The card manager should validate this list with that of the card issuer to ensure that there is a complete list of card holders without any discrepancy. The card manager should also notify the card holders of the dates involved in any change, in particular the date when a card holder might expect a replacement card.

The cards are normally issued by the card issuer directly to the card holder. The procedures should state this and say what should be done if a replacement card is not received.

Withdrawal of a card

The two usual reasons for withdrawing a card are abuse of the card and when a card holder changes job or leaves the procurement organisation.

The procedures should spell out what constitutes abuse of the card. Normally, abuse is one or more of the following:

- breach of financial limits;

- use of non-approved suppliers;

- purchase of non-approved goods and services.

A further source of abuse is the use of the card to purchase items for personal use. This could be done with the intention of reimbursing the procurement organisation with the cost of such goods or services or without this intention in which case the abuse is fraud. Fraud is normally a dismissible offence as well as being a crime. It can be very difficult to know whether fraud is intended when the use of the cards for personal purposes is permitted by the procurement organisation. For this reason, it is best not to permit any personal purchases. The procedures should make it clear that the cards are only to be used for business purposes and that they are not to be used for personal use.

The procedures should also make it clear what the consequences are of any breach of use.

Adding new suppliers

As has been mentioned, it is possible to restrict the use of the card to certain merchant classes of supplier. It is the responsibility of the card user to notify the card manager of the need for a new supplier class. The card manager will need to liaise with the card issuer. This is discussed below. It is also possible that the card may be used for a certain class of supplier but that a particularly useful supplier does not currently accept the card. Again, the card holder should notify the card manager. The procedures should require that notification be done in writing.

If a new class of supplier is required and the procurement organisation already uses suppliers in this class, then the restriction needs to be changed if the suppliers are conveniently located for supply purposes. Otherwise, it will be necessary to vet the suitability of possible suppliers in this class through some pre-qualification process. This should naturally include any suppliers which the card holder has suggested. The procedures should state who will undertake this vetting and the extent to which a full pre-qualification is needed.

It will be necessary for the card issuer (acting in its role of supplier acquirer) to be asked to approach suppliers which do not currently accept the card. The procedures should require the card manager to approach the card issuer with the request for an approach to the supplier to be made. The card issuer should be required to keep the card manager aware of progress. The card manager should keep the card holder advised. The card issuer may wish to vet the supplier itself for its own purposes.

It is generally found to be helpful if the possible new supplier is approached by the procurement organisation and requested to accept the card. This should normally be done by the card holder.

Managing existing suppliers

The card holder should sort out any problems with the supplier regarding delivery, quality and price and thus act as the point of reference for complaints and problems with suppliers. Central procurement departments should only be involved exceptionally in such disputes with the suppliers. The amounts of money involved and the risk to the procurement organisation are both likely to be low. The procedures should only require the involvement of professional purchasing if the dispute cannot be resolved at the local level.

In the event of a supply failure, such as non-delivery or inferior goods etc., a claim for a refund needs to be made to the supplier. The procedures should require the card holder to promptly deal with the supplier and to notify the card manager of any disputed amounts. The procedures should require the card holder to obtain the supplier's consent to the refund being claimed. The supplier should issue a credit via the card issuer.

If this consent is not forthcoming, then the refund should be claimed by the card holder from the card issuer but only when it is certain that the procurement organisation will itself not be in breach of contract by obtaining a refund. The card holder should notify the card manager when the supplier has not consented to the refund and the card manager should satisfy him or herself that the procurement organisation will not be in breach of contract if a refund is claimed.

The procedures should make it plain that goods cannot be returned to a supplier for cash. There is an obvious risk of fraud if this happens. Disregarding this requirement could be the subject of disciplinary action.

Deleting suppliers

For various reasons, it might be necessary to no longer trade with a supplier using a purchasing card. If this situation arises, the card manager should be advised and he or she should issue a general notice to all card users.

If the intention is no longer to trade using purchasing cards with a certain class of supplier, then the card manager should notify the card issuer to block the merchant category code.

Payment of invoices

It is each card holder's responsibility to reconcile purchasing card invoices with the original order for the goods and any information concerning delivery. The information about the order and the delivery should be captured as described above in the section on 'ordering from a supplier'.

Although suppliers are required by card issuers to only make a charge after they have taken steps to deliver the goods or service, there might be occasions when the goods or the service will not be delivered before the payment has been charged by the card issuer. The card issuer will be entitled to payment and the procedures should make it clear that the invoice is to be passed for payment. The card holder should maintain a record of purchases for which payment has been made even though the goods or service have not been received. This can be done on the purchase record sheet described in the section on 'ordering from a supplier'. The progress of the delivery can be monitored using the delivery diary and both the diary and the purchase record sheet should be noted when the delivery has been received.

The extent of reconciliation by the card holder will depend on whether the card issuer invoice is a line item detail invoice or a summary invoice (see section on 'VAT' above). It should be possible to reconcile each individual item on a line item invoice against the purchase record sheet and the delivery diary. This can be a long-winded task if the purchasing cards are used as a means of payment for lots of low-spend orders. When this is the case, the procedures might give a dispensation to reconcile the invoices on an occasional basis, possibly by checking some of the lines and not others or by reconciling some invoices but not others.

If this dispensation is granted, then it should be for audit to ensure that there is no abuse of the use of the card. However, a balance needs to be struck between reverting to almost as much work when reconciling invoices as would occur if a purchasing card were not used and ensuring that the cards are not abused either by employees or by suppliers. Trust is important in business but so is vigilance.

Once the invoice has been reconciled, the procedures should require it to be certified for payment. The procedures should state who may do this. Reconciliation, certification and the original ordering of the goods or services should not be done by the same person. This separation of powers provides a check which could make abuse of the cards more difficult.

Following reconciliation, the invoice is passed to accounts for payment.

Audit

Audits are needed to ensure that the use of purchasing cards is not being abused.

If the above process has been followed when ordering goods/services and when reconciling and certifying the invoice, audit will be relatively straightforward. It should be conducted at random by the audit department of the procurement organisation and by the central procurement department in organisations which use a centralised or centralised/decentralised approach or by the card manager in a decentralised organisation. The audit department and the procurement department/card manager should agree both the frequency of the audits and, of course, they should be conducted at random and without prior notice.

Security

The procedures should require the cards to be kept securely and that card numbers should not be unnecessarily disclosed. Only individuals designated to use a card should place an order requiring payment by means of that card.

CHAPTER 14

E-procurement

Although e-procurement has been available in one form or another for several years now, there is no real agreement about what the term actually means. At one extreme it is used to describe procurement by means of purchasing cards and the use of e-mails to send invitations to tender and receive tenders, invoices, etc. At the other extreme, there is the use of e-auction techniques and the specialist use of 'supply sites' and 'market sites'. Some people would also include the purchase of items off retail websites and others would include purchasing from business-to-business websites, possibly using a purchase card.

The specialist supply and market sites are often offered as part of an enterprise resource planning (ERP) package. They are particularly suitable for the purchase of supplies, i.e. goods for which they usually seem to have been specifically designed. However, they can usually also be used to buy services. Briefly, the supply site covers requisitioning including authorisation as well as inventory management, supplier selection and production of an order. A market site may include sending an invitation to tender to suppliers, receiving a tender, tender analysis, raising and obtaining approval for an order, issuing the order to the supplier and receiving some form of acknowledgement, receiving and tracking the delivery of the goods, updating inventory and managing the invoicing process. The tender analysis is sometimes only a price comparison although some systems compare whole-life cost and they can take account of other factors using a scoring and weighting process not dissimilar to that described elsewhere in this book.

Even before the almost universal use of the Internet, there were IT packages which offered the functionality provided by supply sites. So, this offering is not particularly new although the ability to link up many users, authorisers and procurement specialists is a refinement which technology has made possible only over the last few years.

Market sites are new and have come into prominence with the universality of the Internet. This has permitted easy connectivity of buyers with suppliers. There have been industry-specific sites available to procurement organisations and suppliers in such industries as the automotive, aerospace, construction and others. Not all of these have been successful nor, for that matter, have many of the organisations offering specialist e-site management. With some sites, the consolidation of several organisations' demands has been an objective with the intention of leveraging better prices from suppliers. Organisations need to be particularly careful, if they are using these sites to do this, that they do not infringe competition legislation. It is not always realised that this legislation applies to business buyers as well as to sellers.

E-auctions have been something of a growth industry in procurement. They are also offered as a part of ERP processes or they are offered on a stand-alone basis by e-auction service providers. The latter organisations provide the software to handle the bidding process. They will also identify suppliers and undertake the pre-qualification and qualification process as well as doing work to identify suitable categories of spend for e-auctioning.

Having found suppliers willing to supply and in which there is a high degree of confidence that they can reliably supply the requirement, it is then possible to have an e-auction. Although an e-auction can be a whole-life cost competition, it is usually a price competition. All bidders participate at the same time, usually during a period of an hour or an hour and a half, although there is no technical reason why longer or shorter time periods could not be used. The bidding is conducted electronically. Each bidder is able to log on to the e-auction system and offer prices to supply the previously defined requirement.

It is possible for both the bidders and members of the purchasing organisation to see the bids of all the bidders on a screen via a PC or laptop. The members of the purchasing organisation (and the staff of the e-auction service provider working with the purchasing organisation) know which bidder has placed which bid. Each bidder knows that other bidders have placed bids in competition with their own but they do not know who the other bidders are, although it is not difficult to guess in markets where there are only a few suppliers. Consequently they do not know which bidder has placed which bid, although it may not be difficult to guess that either.

Usually bidders open high and then reduce their prices in competition with one another in an effort to win the business. These price reductions are visible to all. Bidding is often slow to start off with and then, near to the end of the bidding period, there can be a flurry of bids as suppliers compete strenuously with one another to win the business. Some auction systems have a facility to extend the bidding period if a bid has been placed within a certain time before the end of the auction, say five or ten minutes. Suppliers should be made aware of this facility before bidding.

Although it has generally been used for supplies, services are being procured using this technique. Spectacular savings have been claimed for supplies. At one time, it was thought that a downside of what is an aggressive form of tender management would be poorer service from suppliers as they sought to recoup some of the margin which they had surrendered during the auctioning process. However, some studies have claimed that this decline in service levels is not happening.

What is different about e-procurement?

For the purposes of this discussion, e-procurement will be split into five parts (see Figure 14.1), following the description given in the above paragraphs:

- use of e-mails for procurement;

- purchasing off retail websites;

- purchasing from business-to-business websites;

- supply and market sites;

- e-auctions.

The use of purchasing cards has been discussed in some detail in Chapter 13.

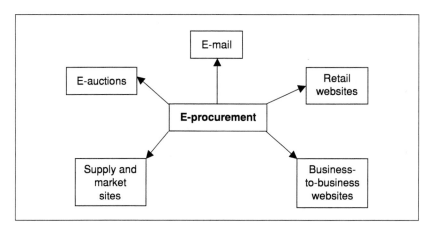

Figure 14.1 E-procurement.

Although much is made of the newness of e-procurement, what needs always to be remembered is that the technology is new but the procurement processes and outcomes are essentially the same as good practices have always been. For example, sending documentation by e-mail, which is now fairly standard practice, simply means that a document arrives more quickly at a recipient than it would have done if it had been sent through the post. The processes to produce documents, their approval prior to issue and their content are not going to be changed because an electronic means of communication is used instead of a paper-based one.

Similarly, purchasing off a retail website is not really different to purchasing from retail premises except that the retail website will probably make sure that the purchase is done on its terms and conditions. The same is true of purchases made from business-to-business type websites.

There are two aspects to consider with respect to supply sites, market sites and e-auctioning. The one which tends to get overlooked is that providers of these services are suppliers like any other. Suppliers of these services often position themselves as fellow procurement professionals and they are also often treated as such by professional procurement bodies, which might rely on them to provide information and conduct research into procurement issues associated with e-procurement. The techniques to identify these suppliers, to pre-qualify them and select them for bidding, to invite and manage bidding, and to evaluate bids, negotiate, place and manage contracts should be exactly the same as those used for any other supplies or services. The applicable procedures are also the same and they have all been described in the preceding chapters of this book.

The second aspect which needs to be considered is the degree to which the procedures described in this book need to be different because the processing is electronic rather than paper based. The various systems might well require a set of instructions and considerable training to manage the software effectively. However, the software should be compatible with the procurement procedures of an organisation, especially if the procedures are intended to ensure a considered approach to procurement which safeguards the organisation and provides a source of strategic competitive advantage.

It is true that supply, market and e-auction systems are often standard packages. This normally means that the procurement organisations adopting them have to bring themselves and their practices in line with the systems and not the other way round, although suppliers of these systems will normally customise them to some (limited) extent to meet the preferences of their clients.

Procurement professionals should be aware of a deviation from best practice procedures and they should make sure that they are not reducing safeguards which are intended to protect the organisation. For example, no instances of collusion between e-auction providers and suppliers have ever been reported but it could happen unless there are adequate safeguards.

Procedures for e-procurement by e-mail

As has been mentioned above, e-mail is simply a way of conveying documents from one organisation to another. It does not alter the content or the intent of the documents. So, all the procedures described in this book should still apply to the generation of the documents and to the requirements placed upon a tenderer or supplier.

For those using English contract law as the legal basis for their contracts, there is, however, one aspect which should be included in any set of procurement procedures. Legally, there are four requirements for a contract. These are:

- offer and acceptance;

- consideration;

- intention to create legal relations;

- capacity to contract.

Assuming that consideration, the intention to create legal relations and the capacity to contract are all in place, a contract comes into being when the acceptance is communicated by the offeree (the organisation receiving an offer) to the offeror (the organisation making an offer).

Since the nineteenth century there has been, in English contract law, a rule that the acceptance is communicated when it is posted even if the actual acceptance is not received by the offeror. This rule, which does not exist in other jurisdictions and which many people would nowadays consider bizarre, does not have an equivalent in electronic communication. In other words, the fact that the offeree has sent an e-mail to the offeror accepting the offer is not sufficient to communicate acceptance. This means that there is no certainty that the acceptance has been communicated simply because an e-mail has been sent.

The procedures should address this point by requiring an e-mailed acceptance to be acknowledged. The best way of doing this is to have the offeror acknowledge by e-mail that the acceptance has been received. This should be an action of the offeror not an automatic response generated by the e-mail system.

Purchasing off retail websites

Terms and conditions will be the key issue for the procedures to address here.

Most retail sites assume that the purchaser is a private individual acting as a consumer and the terms and conditions will be drafted by the retailer so as to minimise its liability to any consumer law. The applicability of consumer law to business-to-business transactions is variable and can be complicated. Also, sites may establish the law of the country in which the retailer is situated as the law governing the contract and the courts of that country as being the ones which will hear any disputes. Both the law and the courts might be different to those of the country of the procurement organisation. It is not normally possible to buy off a retail site without accepting the terms and conditions of the retailer.

In general, most procurements off retail sites will be of low spend value and low risk. The difficulties caused by the retailer stipulating its terms and conditions for the contract are not usually going to be grave for the procurement organisation. It should, however, make sure that it knows what are the terms and conditions applying to any procurement. The procedures should contain a requirement that the terms and conditions are copied and saved or printed off in case reference to them is needed in the future. The procedures should impose a similar requirement to copy and save or print off any screens which show the offer and acceptance.

Purchasing from business-to-business websites

It is convenient to divide procurements off business-to-business websites into two categories:

- infrequent procurements;

- frequent procurements.

For infrequent procurements, the circumstances are similar to those applying to purchasing off retail sites, namely that the procurement is likely to be on the supplier's terms and conditions. Procedural requirements should also be the same with respect to keeping a record of the terms and conditions and any offer and acceptance screens.

For frequent purchases, consideration should be give to putting some sort of framework contract in place with terms and conditions clearly stipulated and not unfavourable to the procurement organisation. There will need to be some clear agreement that these take precedence over the seller's terms and conditions appearing on the website if ordering via the website is to be the way of ordering. If the procurement organisation uses a market site, it would be better to buy by means of the framework agreement using that site and not use the vendor's website at all.

The worst scenario for frequent purchases is that the vendor refuses to deal with the procurement organisation except through the vendor's website and only then on the vendor's terms and conditions. In this case, which should only happen if, for some reason, there is no competition to the vendor, the procurement organisation will have to treat the procurements as if they are all infrequent procurements, i.e. keep copies of the terms and conditions and any offer and acceptance screens.

Supply and market sites

As already mentioned, the procurement organisation should require that these sites conform with its procedures and not that its procedures conform with the workings of these sites.

Often, these sites are sold as a part of an ERP solution and the integration of the procurement process with the inventory and finance processes are sometimes considered more important by top management of a procurement organisation than conformity with good procurement procedures. This might mean some changes to the procedures. However, a considerable part of the work covered by the procedures described in this book cannot be undertaken by an electronic process.

A few moments thought will show that the identification of the need, the translation of this need into a requirement, the ascertaining of the commercial information, and the development of a contract strategy and plan are not normally things which e-procurement systems can do. The same is true of the contract management process. E-systems can undertake the processing part of pre-qualification and qualification and the issuing of the invitation to tender, and they can provide a process for tender evaluation. They can also be used for letting a contract or issuing an order. But the development of criteria for pre-qualification and tender evaluation needs to be undertaken outside the system. Also, even though these systems can hold standard invitations to tender, which will be perfectly satisfactory on many and, in some organisations, possibly most occasions, these should still be reviewed as described in the procedures.

In almost all organisations, there will be procurements for which e-procurement systems can provide not much more than a postal service and all the cerebral work needed to conduct an effective and efficient procurement will still have to be done outside of the system. These will be infrequent, major procurements, such as the construction of a significant new asset.

E-auctions

Procurement specialists should satisfy themselves that the e-auction service providers conform with the procurement organisation's procedures instead of applying their own.

This should be so when the e-auction service provider undertakes the task of spend mapping, categorisation of procurement and pre-qualification of suppliers, and deals with getting the supplier's agreement to the procurement organisation's terms and conditions and confirmation from the supplier that it can meet the specification and will participate in the auction.

CHAPTER 15

European Procurement Directives – introductory comments

The European Procurement Directives apply to all organisations in the public sector and to utilities in the provision of energy (basically electricity), oil and gas, water and transport. There are differences between the Public Sector Directive and the Utilities Directive.

The next two chapters will review in more detail Directive 2004/17/EC for Utilities and Directive 2004/18/EC for the Public Sector which should be implemented into national law by 31 January 2006.

Scope of Chapters 16 and 17

It is not intended in the next two chapters to give a full description of the Directives. Readers are recommended to read the source documents, basically the Directives themselves and the member state legislation which puts them into effect. What is intended is to sketch what should be considered for inclusion in procurement procedures.

Organisations which are not in the public sector or are not utilities or have been exempted for some reason should not be concerned by the content of this chapter or either of the next two chapters as the Directives do not affect them.

Organisations affected by the Directives will probably want to integrate their effects into the appropriate parts of their procedures.

Keep it simple

It is suggested that the simplest approach to the Directives is to apply them if in doubt. It is true that this might cause some delay but nothing which could not be managed with foresight and good planning. It is also suggested that trying to avoid the Directives can involve more work and some risk than simply complying with them.

How the requirements of the Directives should be integrated with the procedures

In the event that a threshold has been exceeded then it might be helpful for there to be a separate set of procedures which take full account of the requirements of the Directives. In effect, this means two separate sets of procedures, one for procurements equal to or lower than the Directives' thresholds and one for those in excess of them. There should of course be considerable overlap and, consequently, there will be a lot of duplication. However, the advantage is that it will be possible to follow the procedures dealing with procurements subject to the Directives in the sure knowledge that compliance with the Directives has been fully addressed.

It will also avoid making cumbersome the procedures for procurement to which the Directives do not apply.

The simplest approach is probably to make the rules on aggregation an early part of the process. The procedures should require the internal customer to contact the procurement agent if the customer thinks that the proposed procurement is likely to exceed the threshold. As a fail-safe, they should also require the procurement agent to check that the relevant Directive does not apply when considering the contract strategy.

Requirements dealing with advertising requirements ('calling for competition') should be a part of the contract plan and should be integrated into the procedures as a precursor to the issue of any invitation to tender. The open, restricted and negotiated processes have all been described in this book and these could be suitable places for the advertising requirements of the Directives to appear.

CHAPTER 16

The Utilities Directive 2004/17/EC

Readers are reminded that this chapter is not intended to be a definitive statement of the contents of the Directive nor an interpretation of it. The chapter's purpose is to indicate what aspects of the Directive should be included in procedures for utilities captured by the Directive. Readers should consult the Directive to incorporate all aspects which they consider necessary into their procedures.

The relevant Directive is 2004/17/EC and it may be downloaded free of charge from:

http://europa.eu.int/comm/internal_market/publicprocurement/ legislation_en.htm

It is also not intended here to deal with the question of which utilities organisations are subject to the Directive. Utilities should consult the Directive to establish whether they are covered or not.

Contracts captured by the Utilities Directive

The Directive defines three types of contract: supply, service and works.

Works contracts cover a range of construction or building activities listed in Annex XII to the Directive or they are contracts for a work which is a building or civil engineering works. *Supply contracts* basically mean the purchase, hire, lease, rental or hire-purchase of goods including any siting or installation. *Service contracts* are contracts other than works or supply contracts. Services are defined in Annex XVII to the Directive and such contracts may include products if these are less than the value of the service. They may also include the works activities in Annex XII if these are incidental to the principal object of the contract, which presumably will be the services themselves.

A definition of these terms is needed in the procedures. Some organisations will also need to include the definitions of a works concession (broadly this occurs when an organisation agrees to build some civil engineering works in return for being able to charge for its use by consumers or other third parties) and a service concession (the principle is similar to a works concession but applies to services).

Only contracts in writing and for a pecuniary interest are captured provided they are over €499,000 for supply and service contracts and €6,242,000 for works contracts, exclusive of VAT in both cases.

Framework agreements may be subject to the Directive, in which case the call-off contracts issued under the framework are not. However, if the framework agreement is let without applying the rules in the Directive, the call-off contracts themselves are subject to the Directive and the rules for aggregation will apply. This seems to be saying that framework agreements should be let in accordance with the Directive and there seems to be no good reason for not doing so.

The Directive now includes the letting of a contract using a 'dynamic purchasing system'. A dynamic purchasing system is defined as a 'complete electronic process for making commonly used purchases'. The definition seems then to describe a market site, discussed in Chapter 14. The Directive specifies a process to be followed when using such a system.

The utility must publish a contract notice (see below for contract notices) advising of the existence of the dynamic purchasing system. The open procedure must be used and any interested party may apply. These parties must be invited to submit an indicative tender against a specification which, among other matters, describes what is to be purchased and information about the electronic purchasing system. The indicative tender can be improved at any time. All of this has to be done electronically and the utility has to grant free access to interested parties to the system. The utility has to evaluate the indicative tender within 15 days from the date of its submission although this timescale may be extended if no invitation to tender is issued before evaluation is complete.

The Directive does not specify that objective criteria should be used for this evaluation of the indicative tender although the contract notice used to announce the existence of the dynamic purchasing system must contain objective criteria for the analysis of the final tenders (see below). On the basis of the evaluation, the interested party can be rejected or become a tenderer for the eventual contract. This contract has to be the subject of an invitation to tender and all those who have passed the test of the indicative tender may tender within a time limit for submission of tenders. The time limit is not specified in the Directive – presumably it will be same as applies for paper-based tendering. The dynamic system may exist for not more than four years except for duly justified exceptional cases but it is not clear whether this means that the contracts may last for this time and then there must be a retendering or whether the dynamic purchasing system should be closed down after this period. The latter seems unlikely.

As has been indicated above, some aspects of the above are in doubt although the broad thrust of ensuring that a market site is open to any potential tenderer to register an interest and to participate in a tender evaluation is clear. Care needs to be given to translate this requirement into procurement procedures and to applying the requirement to a market site.

Aggregation of contract values

The Directive requires the aggregation of contract values (exclusive of VAT) in order to see whether they are equal to or exceed the thresholds. The value is to be the total value including any options and prizes or payments made by the utility to candidates (a candidate being defined as one which has sought an invitation to take part in a restricted or negotiated procedure). Circumvention of the Directives by splitting the value of a contract or failing to aggregate properly is prohibited.

For *framework agreements and dynamic purchasing systems*, the estimated value is the total value of all the contracts to be let for the total term of the agreement/system.

When calculating *the value of works contracts*, the value of any supplies or services necessary for the execution of the works must be included but supplies and services not necessary for the works must not be included. They must be aggregated separately and compared with the supplies/services threshold.

If a works or services are to be purchased as separate lots at the same time, then the value of all the lots must be aggregated but the Directive does then give the right not to apply its rules to lots of value less than €80,000 for services and €1 million for works provided the value of the lots does not exceed 20 per cent of the total value.

A similar rule to that which applies to lots for services also applies *to lots for supplies* if they are to be purchased at the same time. The €80,000 threshold also applies to lots for supplies.

Briefly, *for lots*, the rule is aggregate the value of the lots first, then, if the value is equal to or in excess of the threshold, apply the rules in the Directive to all lots, but it is permissible not to apply them to lots not exceeding the values indicated above.

To calculate *the estimated contract value for supply or service contracts which are regular in nature or which are intended to be renewed within a given period*, the rule is to aggregate the value of all contracts over the past 12 months or financial year and to adjust for likely changes in demand *or* to aggregate over the 12 months following the first delivery or during the financial year if the delivery period is greater than 12 months. The Directive presents these options and it does not say when one or the other may be used. It is suggested that the procedures should require both to be applied if this is possible and, if either of the two methods of calculation equal or exceed the threshold, to apply the rules in the Directive.

When calculating *the value of a single contract for supplies and services*, the values of both the supplies and services must be added together for comparison purposes and any siting and installation costs must also be included.

For *supply contracts which involve leasing, hire, rental or hire purchase*, the value is the total value including any estimated residual value for fixed-term contracts if the period of the agreement exceeds 12 months but it is the total value for the period of the agreement if it is less than 12 months. Where there is no fixed term, aggregation is to be done by multiplying the monthly value by 48.

For *insurance services*, the value is the premium and fees payable. For *banking and other financial services* (but note that the issue, purchase, sale and transfer of securities and other financial instruments are excluded as are transactions to raise money or capital), the value is the total of fees, commissions and other remuneration.

For *contracts involving design tasks*, the value is also the fees, commissions and other remuneration.

For *service contracts with a contract period of less than 48 months*, the value is the fee for the contract period. If there is no contract period or it is longer than 48 months, then it is the monthly value multiplied by 48.

These rules need to be included in the procurement procedures.

Excluded contracts

Certain contracts are excluded from the Directive. The reader is recommended to consult the Directive for a list of these.

Reserved contracts and contracts awarded by a central body

The Directive also contains provision for member states to ensure the right to participate of sheltered workshops in contract award procedures, in which case the call for competition has to refer to Article 28 of the Directive.

Should a member state introduce this provision, then the procedures will have to ensure that sheltered workshops are given the opportunity to participate.

The Directive also permits member states to require utilities to purchase through a central body. If this happens, then the procedures will have to make it clear when such purchasing should take place.

Rules for utilities to seek exemption from the Directive

There are rules which permit a utility to seek exemption from the Directive. This is not really an issue for procurement procedures. Article 30 of the Directive applies.

Rules applying to services

Annex XVIIA lists services to which the rules of the Directives apply. Services listed in Annex XVIIB are subject to the rules about technical specifications and the rules about contract award notices. If the contract is for services which fall into both annexes, then the contract is to be treated as for Annex XVIIA services if those services make up the greater spend of the contract, and as Annex XVIIB services if this is not true.

This is an important point and should appear in the procedures.

Technical specifications

The definitions of technical specifications for services and supplies as well as for works are extremely comprehensive but unlikely to cause any surprise. It is noteworthy that packaging requirements, environmental aspects, safety and accessibility for disabled persons are all included.

Standards are defined as international (from an international standards body), European (adopted by a European standards organisation) and national (adopted by a national standards body).

There are also definitions of European technical approval, common technical specifications and technical reference.

All definitions are contained in Annex XXI.

Article 34 of the Directive requires standards to be set out in contract notices, contract documents or additional documents (whatever the latter may be). They are specifically required to take account of accessibility for the disabled and to design for all users. They are also required not to discriminate against tenderers.

Unless there are legally binding national rules which are compatible with Community law, technical specifications are required to refer in order of preference to national standards transposing European standards, European technical approvals, common technical standards, and international standards or other technical reference systems established by European standardisation bodies. Only when no part of this hierarchy exists may national standards, national technical approvals or national technical specifications be invoked. All references are required to be accompanied by the words 'or equivalent'.

As an alternative to the references mentioned in the above paragraph, the technical specification may be a performance specification including environmental considerations provided the performance specification is sufficiently detailed to ensure that the tenderers know what is required. If required, the performance specification may refer to a part of the detailed hierarchy of standards mentioned above. The other possibility is to refer to the standards for some parts of the specification and to the performance for others.

There are further rules which prevent a utility from rejecting a tender because of apparent failure by the tenderer to conform with the literal wording of the specification requirement if the tenderer can prove by means of a technical dossier from a manufacturer or a test report from a recognised body that the tenderer has in fact complied with the specification.

There are also rules for environmental characteristics as part of a performance specification. Basically, European or multinational eco-labels may be used subject to certain safeguards.

There is a rule requiring that makes or sources are not restrictively defined so that only a supplier or certain suppliers are favoured. The rule also includes not specifying processes, trade marks, patents, types or a particular origin or production process if this eliminates or favours certain organisations or their products. If it is exceptionally needed to use any of these methods of specifying a requirement, the words 'or equivalent' must be used.

Utilities are required to make specifications available on request or to refer to documents which are readily available.

It is obvious from the above abbreviated description that the procedures need to make clear what is and what is not allowed. Readers are advised to study the contents of the Directive carefully before writing these into the procedures. The obvious place for them to go is described in Chapter 6.

Variants

Variants are optional offers made by a supplier which may not strictly conform with all the technical aspects of a specification but which might still meet a utility's requirement.

They may be considered if the award of a contract is based on the most economically advantageous tender and if the specification said that variants were permissible and, if so, what the minimum requirements for the variant should be.

It is not permitted to reject a variant because to accept it would mean accepting a service contract instead of a supply contract or vice versa.

These would be included under the heading 'Requirements' in Chapter 6.

Subcontracting and conditions for performance of contracts

Utilities may ask in contract documents or be required to ask by the member state for details of the share of a contract which is to be subcontracted and who the subcontractors may be.

Utilities may also specify special conditions about the performance of a contract subject to these being in conformance with Community law. They must be specified in the call for competition or in the specification. The special conditions may include social or environmental concerns.

There would only be a need to refer to these in the procedures if a utility either had to or wanted to comply with these requirements.

Obligations relating to taxes, environmental protection, employment protection provisions and working conditions

The body or bodies from which a tenderer may obtain information about these matters may be stated (or required by the member state to be stated) in the contract documents. If this information is supplied, then the utility has to request tenderers to confirm in their tenders that they have taken these matters into account.

Once again, this only needs to be included in the procedures if the utility is obliged by the member state to comply or if it wants to comply.

Procedures

There are only certain circumstances when a tender may be sought without a prior call for competition and all of these will have to be mentioned in the procedures. Briefly, these circumstances exist if:

- there are no tenders or suitable tenders or no applications in response to a prior call for competition. Any contract to be placed must remain substantially the same as that advertised;

- the contract is purely for research, experiment, study or development and not for profit or recovering costs of research or development;

- the contract can only be undertaken by one supplier because of technical or artistic reasons or for reasons connected with the protection of an exclusive right;

- there is urgency owing to unforeseeable events;

- additional deliveries are required from the existing supplier either to partially replace normal supplies or installations or they are required in addition to existing supplies or installations and only they will do because of compatibility problems;

- additional works or services, which were not originally specified, are now needed owing to unforeseen circumstances. They have to be awarded to the original contractor but only if they cannot be separated from the main works or services without great inconvenience or, if they can be separated, they have to be strictly necessary for the later stages of the contract for the original works or services;

- new works are required which are a repetition of existing works 'provided that such works conform to a basic project for which a first contract was awarded after a call for competition'. Notice has to be given that this may be done and the cost of these new works has to be taken into account for aggregation purposes;

- the requirements are call-off contracts under a framework agreement;

- the purchases are bargain purchases, i.e. items bought at temporarily available low prices;

- the purchases are supplies from organisations which are winding up, going into liquidation, are bankrupt, etc.;

- the contract is a service contract which is awarded following a design contract organised in accordance with the Directive. If awarded to one of the winners of the contest, all winners have to be invited to negotiate.

If none of the above apply, contracts have to be let in accordance with one of the open, restricted or negotiated procedures.

It would probably be best if there is a separate section in a utility's procedures which deals with a call for competition and the above exceptions, when a call for competition is not needed, are included in this section.

Periodic indicative notices

In the separate section mentioned immediately above, the procedures will have to describe the notices which need to be placed in order to

---

call for competition. The notices must be sent to the Commission's Office for the Official Publications of the European Communities in a specified format. They may also be published on a buyer profile.

The periodic indicative notice is a notice to be published annually for supplies whose aggregated value for a contract area (obtained by referring to the common procurement vocabulary (CPV) nomenclature as described in the Directive) is equal to or greater than €750,000. The same annual threshold applies to services but only to the categories which appear in Annex XVIIA to which the rules of the Directives apply. The notices for supplies and services have to be sent to the Commission or published on a buyer profile as soon as possible after the start of a budgetary year.

For works and for framework agreements, the annual threshold is €6,242,000. These notices have to be sent to the Commission or published on the buyer profile as soon as possible after the decision approving the planning of the works or framework agreements.

The periodic indicative notice is required for 12 months' requirements looking forward. There are rules about their format and notices published on buyer profiles have to be forwarded electronically to the Commission.

It is possible for procurement organisations to reduce the compulsory periods for tendering provided they have published a periodic indicative notice.

If a previous detailed periodic indicative notice has been published, any further periodic indicative notices for that project do not have to repeat all the detail provided they refer to the previous notice.

Notices for qualification systems

If procurement organisations wish to use a qualification system (to be described later), then they have to publish a notice advertising its existence. This notice has to be published annually if the system is to last longer than three years. Its format is specified in the Directive.

Notices for a call for competition

The procedures will need to make clear that a call for competition may be made by means of a periodic indicative notice or by means of a qualification system notice or by means of a contract notice.

The format for contract notices is specified in the Directive and there is a different format if a dynamic purchasing system is to be used, i.e. procurement is to be done electronically.

If the periodic indicative notice is being used as a call for competition, it has to specifically refer to the supplies, services or works concerned, state whether the open, restricted or negotiated procedure will be used and state that there will be no further calls for competition. This notice has to be published not more than 12 months before organisations expressing an interest in tendering/negotiating for the contract are invited to confirm their interest.

Contract award notices

The procedures must require this notice to be published within two months of the award of a contract or framework agreement. For dynamic purchasing systems, the notices may be grouped quarterly but the grouped notice must be sent within two months of the end of the quarter.

The procedures must make clear that the contract award notice is in a format defined in the Directive and that confidential aspects must be pointed out to the Commission.

It is possible to limit the amount of information given when announcing the award of contracts for research and development purposes. This depends on whether the contract was let without a call for competition and whether a periodic indicative notice or a qualification system notice was published.

Form and manner of publication of notices

The Directive specifies the information to be included in the various notices and says that they might be sent electronically by accessing the preferred format at *http://simap.eu.int* or by other means. If sent electronically using the preferred format, publication is promised within five days of the notice being sent; otherwise it is within 12 days but this can be five days in exceptional circumstances provided the notice is sent by fax.

Notices are published in an official language of the Community and it is the procurement organisation which selects the language.

The procedures will need to make it clear that notices cannot be published nationally before the date they are sent to the Commission and national notices cannot contain information different to that sent to the Commission or published on a buyer profile. They have to mention the date of dispatch to the Commission or the date of publication on the buyer profile.

The procedures will also need to make it clear that periodic indicative notices cannot be published on a buyer profile before dispatch to the Commission and again the date of their dispatch must be stated.

It will also be necessary for the procedures to state how the procurement organisation will prove that it has sent the notices to the Commission and how the procurement organisation will deal with the confirmation of publication from the Commission.

Time limits

The Directive specifies time limits for the receipt of tenders in the open procedure and for receipt of requests to participate in the restricted and negotiated procedures. There is a general requirement to allow sufficient time and to take account of complexity.

For the open procedure, the minimum time limit for receipt of tenders is 52 days from the date of dispatch of the contract notice.

For restricted and negotiated procedures, the time limit for a request to participate should normally be not less than 37 days from the date when a contract notice was sent or an invitation to confirm interest was sent to those suppliers which had responded to a periodic indicative notice acting as a call for competition. In unspecified circumstances, the Directive permits this to be reduced to 22 days if the notice was sent other than electronically or by fax and to 15 days if electronic transmission or fax were used.

The procedures will need to stipulate these time limits.

The procedures must also deal with the requirement that the time limit for tenders may be set by mutual agreement with the selected tenderers (which includes those suppliers with which the procurement organisation will negotiate if following the negotiated procedure) but all tenderers must have the same time to prepare and submit their tenders. If agreement about the period cannot be reached, then the Directive fixes the period at 24 days but says that it may in no circumstances be less than ten days from the date of invitation to tender.

If a periodic indicative notice has been used as a call for competition, the minimum time limit for receipt of tenders is not less than 36 days in the open procedure but this may be reduced to 22 days provided much more information has been given in the periodic indicative notice. It is also conditional on the periodic indicative notice having been sent for publication between 52 days and 12 months before the date on which the contract notice is sent.

It is possible to further reduce by seven days the time periods for requests to participate in restricted and negotiated procedures or for receipt of tenders in the open procedure if notices have been drawn up and transmitted electronically in the preferred format mentioned above.

A further five days reduction is possible for receipt of tenders in the open, restricted and negotiated procedures if the tenderer has 'unrestricted and full direct access' to all the invitation to tender documentation exhibited on the procurement organisation's website. This access is to be from the date on which the call for competition is published and this has to specify the Internet address from which the documentation may be downloaded.

These time limits and the various reductions need to be carefully explained in the procedures. The procedures must limit the extent of the reductions so that at least 15 days must be allowed for tendering from the date of dispatch of the contract notice in the open procedure provided this has been sent by fax or electronic means. If it has not been sent in either of these ways, the limit is 22 days.

For restricted and negotiated procedures, the time limits must not be less than 15 days for requests to participate. The time limit is ten days for receipt of tenders unless a lower time limit is agreed mutually by the procurement organisation with the suppliers who will be tendering.

If there has been some delay in issuing the invitation to tender or any supporting documents which have been requested in accordance with the time limits imposed by the Directives, or if a site visit is needed or inspection of documents at some site is needed, then the time limits for receipt of tenders must be extended unless a time limit has been set by mutual agreement.

In an effort to promote understanding of what is a very complicated article (Article 45) in the Directive, the Commission has provided a summary in Annex XXII.

Any procedures will need to carefully explain the various options and it might be that it will be easier to set simplified time limits which are higher than the lower limits set in the Directives. This would avoid breach even if it did not take advantage of the choices offered in the Directive.

If this is not acceptable, care needs to be taken on many fronts. For example, the Directive refers to mutual agreement of time for tendering. Such timing is not normally mutually agreed. Usually, the procurement organisation specifies a time period and suppliers are required to comply with it. After tenders have been invited, a supplier might ask for an extension to the time period, which might or might not be granted. Thought should now be given to obtaining from tenderers a confirmation that the time limit specified in an invitation to tender is acceptable to them. Some of the features of timing depend on this mutual agreement.

Two further timing features with the open procedure are the requirement to issue specifications and supporting documentation to suppliers within six days of their being requested if they are not available electronically, presumably by accessing the documents on the procurement organisation's website. The request for the documentation has to be received in good time before the time limit for submission of tenders. This is presumably six days before the date for submission of tenders as any additional information requested by the supplier must be provided not later than six days before the time limit fixed for receipt of tenders.

Invitations to submit a tender or to negotiate

Article 47 of the Directive deals with the issue of invitation to tender documentation or invitations to negotiate. The Directive requires the simultaneous issue of such invitations as well as advice about where to obtain specifications and supporting documentation if such documentation is not part of any invitation. Any additional information has to be sent within six days before the final date for receipt of tenders, provided it is requested in good time.

The Directive also requires that the invitation to tender specifies the time limit for requesting documents and any payment for them, the final date for receipt of tenders, the address to which they are to be sent and the language(s) to be used. It also requires a reference to the contract notice, an indication of any documents attached, details of the contract award criteria and the weightings or importance of such criteria if none of this information has been advised in a notice about a qualification system when used as a call for competition.

When the periodic indicative notice is used as a call for competition, the Directive lists a range of information which must be included in an invitation to suppliers who respond to such a notice. This invitation is made so that the suppliers may confirm their interest in tendering or negotiating. The information, which should be listed in the procedures, is:

- nature and quantity (nature presumably means the kind of requirement) including information about options (for works and services, information about their nature and quantity and estimated publication dates of any notices for competition for works, supplies or services);

- whether restricted or negotiated procedure is to be used;

- date of delivery of supplies or execution of works or services;

- address and closing dates for any request for invitations to tender and the applicable language of these documents;

- address of the entity to award the contract;

- economic and technical conditions, financial guarantees, etc.;

- details of amount and procedures for buying the invitation to tender if applicable;

- whether the invitation is for a tender for a purchase contract, a hire contract, a lease or hire purchase or some combination;

- contract award criteria and weightings or importance as applicable provided this information is not provided in the periodic indicative notice, nor in the specifications nor the invitation to tender or negotiate.

Communication and information

Some consideration might be necessary about how much of this Article 48 needs to be included in the procedures. The Article permits the use of the customary means of communication provided they do not hinder communication, ensure integrity of documentation and confidentiality and require the procurement organisation to look at tenders only after the expiry date for their return.

The Article deals with the nature of electronic systems but these are unlikely to be issues dealt with in procurement procedures.

The procedures will probably need to deal with the following. The Article describes requests to participate and how they should be transmitted. It permits requests to participate by telephone but requires them to be confirmed in writing before the time limit set for expiry of their receipt. The Article also permits the procurement organisation to request that faxed requests to participate are confirmed in writing by post or by electronic means 'if this is necessary for the purposes of legal proof'. This requirement has to be stated in the call for competition or in the invitation to confirm interest sent to those responding to a periodic indicative notice used as a call for competition.

Information to applicants for qualification, candidates and tenderers

The following aspects would have to be included in the procedures.

Procurement organisations are required to let suppliers know, in writing if requested, of the decisions regarding the letting of a contract or framework agreement or admission to a dynamic purchasing system. This applies whether the decision is to award or not to award or not to implement a dynamic system or to recommence a procedure to seek tenders.

Procurement organisations have to provide suppliers on request with the reasons for the rejection of their application to be considered for bidding. Procurement organisations also have to advise unsuccessful tenderers why their tenders have been rejected, particularly if the rejection is to do with specification issues. Any unsuccessful tenderer who made an admissible tender has to be told of the 'characteristics and relative advantages of the tender selected' and be given the name of the successful tenderer or parties to the framework agreement. Fifteen days maximum is allowed to provide this information from receipt of a written request. The only exceptions to giving this information are grounds which are to do with impeding law enforcement or grounds that disclosure would be contrary to the public interest or prejudice the legitimate commercial interests of a third party.

This Article also introduces qualification. There is no distinction between pre-qualification and qualification in the Directive. The procedures will have to require a decision about pre-qualifying (as described in this book) a supplier within six months presumably from an application to be pre-qualified. If the decision will take longer than four months from the application, the procurement organisation must inform the applicant within two months of the application and give reasons and a date when the application will be accepted or rejected. This suggests that the procurement organisation knows from the start that it will take longer than four months. A rejected applicant has to be advised within 15 days of the date of the decision and the decision must be based on the pre-qualification criteria (the Directive calls them the qualification criteria). The Directive also stipulates that a supplier's approval may only be terminated on the basis of these criteria. This means that a supplier may only be removed from an approved suppliers list on this basis. The supplier has to be informed of the reasons in writing and not later than 15 days before the removal from the list.

All of this clearly has a bearing on how both pre-qualification and qualification are undertaken and should be included in the procedures dealing with these aspects.

Information to be stored concerning awards

Procurement organisations are required to keep information for at least four years which will enable them to justify their decisions about qualification and selection of suppliers and award of contracts, the use of procedures without a call for competition and information about the non-applicability of the Directive. The procedures will have to reflect these requirements.

Conduct of a procedure

This part of the Directive deals with pre-qualification, which the Directive unfortunately calls 'qualification'. This word will be used from now on and the word pre-qualification will be added in brackets in order to refer to the designation used in this book and in common parlance among procurement specialists. The Directive uses the expression 'qualitative selection' to describe the process called qualification in this book and among procurement specialists. We will use qualitative selection but put the word qualification in brackets behind it to refer to the chapter describing the qualification process in this book.

This part of the Directive also deals with contract award criteria, the use of electronic auctions, abnormally low tenders and various aspects of tenders from third countries, i.e. countries with which there is no EU agreement that companies in the EU may have free access to those countries' markets.

Qualification (pre-qualification)

Qualification (pre-qualification) only applies to the restricted and negotiated procedures. If it is used as a call for competition, then suppliers to be invited to tender or negotiate must be selected from the qualified (pre-qualified) suppliers. A qualification notice has to be used to call for competition and the notice has to comply with Annex XIV of the Directive. The notice has to be published annually if the qualification (pre-qualification) approval is to last for more than three years.

The procedures should make it clear that suppliers interested in becoming qualified (pre-qualified) may apply at any time and that qualification (pre-qualification) shall be applied on the basis of objective criteria and rules. If technical criteria are to be some of those criteria, then rules in the Directive about technical specifications must apply (see section on technical specifications above). Updating of the criteria and rules is permissible.

Referring to Article 45 of the Public Sector Directive 2004/18/ EC, the Utilities Directive permits the rules in that Article to be used to disqualify any supplier from being qualified (pre-qualified). These rules include: participation in a criminal organisation, corruption, fraud, money laundering, various forms of financial distress such as bankruptcy or being wound up or affairs administered by a court etc., professional misconduct, failure to fulfil tax and social security obligations and guilt of misrepresentation. Readers should refer to the Public Sector Directive for the details concerning each exclusion and the evidence needed to justify the exclusion.

The Directive permits a supplier to rely on the financial and technical support of other entities and, presumably, to offer these as if they were its own capability provided the supplier can prove that these capabilities will be available to it during the course of any proposed contract.

All the rules and criteria of qualification (pre-qualification) have to be communicated to the interested suppliers on request and any changes have to be notified to those which might be affected. It is possible for a procurement organisation to rely on some other organisation's qualification (pre-qualification) process and not to undertake the work of qualification (pre-qualification) itself. In this case, the procurement organisation has to tell interested suppliers the name of the other organisation.

The Directive requires a written copy of the approved suppliers list divided into categories according to the type of contract which might be let.

When undertaking qualification (pre-qualification), it is not permissible to impose administrative, technical or financial conditions on some suppliers which would not be imposed on others. It is also not permissible to require tests or evidence which would duplicate objective evidence with is already available. If the procurement organisation wants certificates which demonstrate compliance with quality assurance standards, then there has to be reference to European standards and certification by bodies conforming to European standards. Equivalent certificates issued by other member states have to be recognised.

If the environmental credentials of works or service providers is to form a part of the qualification (pre-qualification), then certificates 'referring to EMAS or to environmental management standards based on European or international standards certified by bodies conforming to Community law or relevant European or international standards' must be accepted. Equivalent certificates from other member states must also be accepted or 'other evidence of equivalent environmental management measures from economic operators'.

Criteria for qualitative selection (qualification)

Selection may also apply to suppliers responding to an open procedure call for competition. Irrespective of whether the qualification is for the open, restricted or negotiated procedures, the criteria and rules used must be objective and available to interested parties.

With restricted and negotiated procedures, it is permissible to reduce the number of suppliers to be invited to tender or negotiate and to use the objective rules and criteria for this purpose provided there is adequate competition.

Once more there is a reference to Article 45 of Public Sector Directive 2004/18/EC regarding use of the rules contained there for selection (see section above on qualification (pre-qualification)).

It is again permissible for a supplier to rely on the technical and financial capacity of another party or other parties and the selection criteria may not discriminate because of this provided the supplier can prove that this relationship is dependable.

Contract award criteria

The procedures will have to stipulate that the only two criteria which may be used to award contracts are lowest price and most economically advantageous tender.

The procedures will also have to make it clear that the latter is to be based on objective criteria which have, in turn, to be based on the subject matter of the contract such as delivery or completion date, running costs, cost-effectiveness, quality, etc. The list in the Directive is quite extensive and would it would seem that it is not intended to be exhaustive. However, the procedures should emphasise that they have to be justified by the nature of the contract and criteria which are not relevant to the contract should not be used.

The procedures may require the use of weightings to be applied to the criteria.

The criteria for most economically advantageous and the range and approximate maximum spread of the weightings must be specified in the call for competition or in the invitation to confirm interest made to those who responded to a periodic indicative notice used as a call for competition. Alternatively, they may be included in the invitation to tender or negotiate or in specifications.

If weightings cannot be specified, then the descending order of importance of the criteria must be specified.

Use of electronic auctions

Subject to member states permitting their use, electronic auctions may be used provided the contract specifications can be established with precision. The basis for an award of a contract using an electronic auction is permitted by the Directive to be lowest price or price and/or 'new values of the features of the tenders indicated in the specification'. This seems to be based on an understanding that the auction will not simply be changes in prices but might be changes in other quantifiable 'values'. The Directive does not make it clear what these might be.

The procedures must require that the call for competition says that an electronic auction is to be used.

The Directive then says that 'the specification shall include' various details. It is not clear whether this specification is to be included in the call for competition or issued subsequently to interested parties. The details are features to do with the electronic auction provided these are quantifiable into figures or percentages, limits on any submittable values stipulated in the specification, information to be made available to tenderers during the course of the auction and when it will be made available, information about the auction process, conditions of bidding and especially the amount by which bids can be reduced, and information about the equipment to be used for bidding and its connection to the bidding system. The procedures must address these requirements.

The procedures must require a full evaluation of any tenders submitted prior to the auction. The evaluation will be concerned with the application of award criteria and their weightings to those parts of the tender which are not going to be a part of the auction. This evaluation can be used as a basis for selecting bidders in the auction, all of which must be simultaneously invited to participate in the auction. The invitation must contain all relevant information about how to connect to the auction and when the auction will start (date and time). The auction may not take place less than two days from the date when the invitation was issued.

The invitation must also give full details of the evaluation of the tenders and its outcome. As mentioned above, this evaluation may be used to select bidders in the electronic auction. The invitation must also state any mathematical formula to be used to rank bids during the auction. Presumably, this formula will take account of price changes, changes to the values which are being bid as well as any rankings/weightings arrived at from the pre-auction evaluation. A separate formula has to be provided for each variant, if variants are permitted.

For the sake of certainty, procedures will have to describe the processes mentioned in the above paragraphs.

The procedures must make it clear that the names of the bidders in an electronic auction may not be disclosed but it is permissible to provide all the information which is usually provided in an auction. The procurement organisation will have to provide instantaneously to all bidders enough information so that the bidders can ascertain at any point in time their relative ranking, i.e. how well they are doing in the auction.

The procedures will also have to state the three ways permitted by the Directives for closing an auction. These include a date and time specified in the invitation to take part in the auction, or when no new prices or new values are received provided the procurement organisation has stated in the invitation how long it will allow after receiving the last bid before it closes the auction, or, finally, when all the stages of the auction as specified in the invitation have been completed. A timetable has to be indicated in the invitation if close-down of the auction is to be after completion of the stages even if this is associated in some way with there being no further new prices.

Abnormally low tenders

The procedures will have to require the procurement organisation to contact in writing each supplier offering an abnormally low tender to request details of 'the constituent elements of the tender which it considers relevant'. There is a list in the Directive of the details which may be covered in the request but this is presumably not intended to be exhaustive. The procurement organisation has to 'verify these constituent elements by consulting the tenderer'. There is nothing to say what this means. Presumably the procurement organisation has to satisfy itself that the information given is genuine and that the bid is supported by the evidence provided by the supplier.

If the abnormally low tender is because of illegal state aid, the procurement agent may reject the bid and must inform the Commission. The supplier has to be given enough time to prove that the aid is legal.

Tenders about products originating in third countries

The procedures might need to note the fact that a procurement organisation is obliged to reject tenders which have more than 50 per cent of the products originating from third countries if there is an equivalent bid which does not meet this criterion, i.e. a tender which has less than 50 per cent of the products originating from a third country. The third countries concerned are those with which the EU does not have an agreement ensuring comparable and effective access of EU suppliers to the third country's market.

Equivalence is defined as a 3 per cent price difference.

Procurement organisations may reject bids which meet the 50 per cent criterion even if they are more than 3 per cent cheaper than the nearest bid which does not meet this criterion but the procurement organisation does not have to do so.

Rules governing service design contests

Design contests have to be open to all organisations or persons in the EU.

The procedures will have to state the threshold. This is an amount equal to or greater than €499,000 which is the value net of VAT of a proposed contract for which the design contest is a precursor. The value of any prizes or payments must be included when calculating the threshold. The rules also apply to design contests the value of whose prizes and payments net of VAT is equal to or greater than €499,000. This is presumably to capture design contests which might not result in a contract.

Certain design contests are excluded from the ambit of the Directive. Basically, these are design contests to do with an activity not captured by the Directive, or an activity in a non-EU country, or an activity or contract which is declared secret by the member state, or which requires special security measures as legally required by the member state, or which are to do with contracts pursuant to international rules. Design contests are also not included if there is competition in the field of the utility concerned. This is a complex issue and the Directive should be consulted.

The procedures will have to require a call for competition using the contest notice in Annex XVIII. The results of a design contest must be announced using the notice contained in Annex XIX. The rules about the issue of notices apply. A notice of the results of the design contest must be forwarded to the Commission within two months of the closure of the design contest. More details are given about this in the Directive.

The Directive requires that the rules of any design contest are adapted to the provisions of the Directive. The procedures must address how this is to be done. In particular, the selection of candidates to participate in a design contest must be done using non-discriminatory selection criteria and there must be sufficient candidates to ensure competition.

The procedures will have to require that the jury is independent of the participants in any contest and that at least a third of the jury have the same qualification as any required of the participants. The jury has to be independent in its decision-making and the jury, when examining plans and projects, must not know from which participant they have come.

The procedures must require the jury to produce a report which shall rank the projects and make any comments and points requiring clarification. The report has to be signed by the members of the jury.

Candidates may be invited to answer questions and minutes of such meetings must be made.

CHAPTER 17

The Public Sector Directive 2004/18/EC

Readers are reminded that this chapter is not intended to be a definitive statement of the contents of the Directive nor an interpretation of it. The chapter's purpose is to indicate what aspects of the Directive need to be considered in procedures for public sector organisations. Readers should consult the Directive and incorporate all aspects which they consider necessary into their procedures.

The relevant Directive is 2004/18/EC and it may be downloaded free of charge from:

http://europa.eu.int/comm/internal_market/publicprocurement/ legislation_en.htm

It is not intended here to deal with the question of whether a public sector organisation is subject to the Directive or not. Public sector organisations should consult the Directive to establish whether they are covered or not.

Contracts captured by the Public Sector Directive

The Directive defines three types of contract: public supply contracts, public service contracts and public works contracts.

Public works contracts cover a range of construction or building activities listed in Annex I to the Directive or they are contracts for a work which is a building or civil engineering works. *Public supply* contracts basically mean the purchase, hire, lease, rental or hire-purchase of goods including any siting or installation. *Public service* contracts are contracts other than works or supply contracts. Services are defined in Annex II to the Directive and such contracts may include products if these are less than the value of the service. They may also include the works activities in Annex I if these are incidental to the principal object of the contract, which presumably will be the services themselves.

A definition of these terms is needed in the procedures. Some organisations will also need to include the definitions of a public works concession (broadly this occurs when an organisation agrees to build some civil engineering works in return for being able to charge for its use by consumers or other third parties) and a service concession (the principle is similar to a works concession but applies to services).

Only contracts in writing and for a pecuniary interest are captured provided they are over certain thresholds which depend on the type of procurement organisation (which the Directive calls a contracting authority).

For organisations listed in Annex IV, basically central government ministries and the bodies which they directly control, the threshold is €162,000 for supply and service contracts and €6,242,000 for works contracts, exclusive of VAT in both cases. The exception is central government bodies in the field of defence which must only apply the Directive to products covered by Annex V.

The threshold is €249,000 for supply and service contracts and €6,242,000 for all parts of the public sector not covered by Annex IV. These thresholds also apply to organisations listed in Annex IV which operate in the field of defence provided the contracts are not covered by Annex V. These thresholds also apply to public service contracts awarded by any public sector procurement organisation for services listed in Category 8 of Annex IIA (Research and development services) and Category 5 (Telecommunications services), 'the positions of which in the CPV are equivalent to CPC reference Nos 7524, 7525 and 7526 and/or the services listed in Annex IIB'.

The Directive also applies if a public sector organisation directly subsidises a contract by another organisation by more than 50 per cent of the threshold for works contracts or of the threshold of €249,000 for service contracts connected to a works.

The applicability rules of the Directive are complex and the annexes are long. Procurement organisations in the public sector are recommended to study the Directive and to incorporate the rules into their procedures to ensure that they apply the rules correctly.

Aggregation of contract values

The Directive requires the aggregation of contract values (exclusive of VAT) in order to see whether they are equal to or exceed the thresholds. The value is to be the total value including any options and prizes or payments made by the public sector organisation to candidates (a candidate being defined as one which has sought an invitation to take part in a restricted or negotiated procedure). Circumvention of the Directive by splitting the value of a contract or failing to aggregate properly is prohibited.

For framework agreements and dynamic purchasing systems, the estimated value is the total value of all the contracts to be let for the total term of the agreement/system.

When calculating the value of works contracts, the value of any supplies or services necessary for the execution of the works must be included but supplies and services not necessary for the works must not be included. They must be aggregated separately and compared with the supplies/services threshold.

If the works or services are to be purchased as separate lots at the same time then the value of all the lots must be aggregated, but the Directive does then give the right not to apply its rules to lots of value less than €80,000 for services and €1 million for works provided the value of the lots does not exceed 20 per cent of the total value. The rule for lots also applies to supplies if they are to be purchased as lots at the same time. Briefly, the rule is: aggregate the value of the lots first; then, if the value is equal to or in excess of the threshold, apply the rules in the Directive to all lots, but it is permissible not to apply them to lots not exceeding the values indicated above.

To calculate the estimated contract value for supply or service contracts which are regular in nature or which are intended to be renewed within a given period, the rule is to aggregate the value of all contracts over the past 12 months or financial year and to adjust for likely changes in demand *or* to aggregate over the 12 months following the first delivery or during the financial year if the delivery period is greater than 12 months. The Directive says that the choice of method of aggregation may not be made so as to exclude the contract from the Directive's rules. It is suggested that the procedures should require both to be applied if this is possible and, if either of the two methods of calculation equal or exceed the threshold, to apply the rules in the Directive.

When calculating the value of a contract for supplies and services, the values of both the supplies and the services must be added together for comparison purposes and siting and installation costs must both be included.

For supply contracts which involve leasing, hire, rental or hire-purchase, the value is the total value including any estimated residual value for fixed-term contracts if the period of the agreement exceeds 12 months and for the period of the agreement if it is less than 12 months. Where there is no fixed term, aggregation is to be done by multiplying the monthly value by 48.

For insurance services, the value is the premium and fees payable. For banking and other financial services (but note that the issue, purchase, sale and transfer of securities and other financial instruments are excluded as are transactions to raise money or capital), the value is the total of fees, commissions and other remuneration. For design contracts, the value is also the fees, commissions and other remuneration.

For service contracts with a contract period of less than 48 months, the value is the fee for the contract period. If there is no contract period or it is longer than 48 months, then it is the monthly value multiplied by 48.

These rules need to be included in the procurement procedures.

Excluded contracts

Certain contracts are excluded from the Directive. The reader is advised to consult the Directive about these.

Reserved contracts

The Directive also contains provision for member states to ensure the right to participate of sheltered workshops in contract award procedures, in which case the call for competition has to refer to Article 19 of the Directive.

Contracts and frameworks awarded by a central body

The Directive also permits member states to require public sector organisations to purchase through a central body providing the central body complies with the Directive.

Rules applying to services

Annex IIA lists services to which the rules of the Directives apply. Services listed in Annex IIB are subject to the rules about technical specifications and the rules about contract award notices. If the contract is for services which fall into both annexes, then the contract is to be treated as for Annex IIA services if those services make up the greater value of the contract and as Annex IIB services if this is not true.

This is an important point and should appear in the procedures.

Technical specifications

The definitions of technical specifications for services and supplies as well as for works are extremely comprehensive. It is noteworthy that packaging requirements, environmental aspects, safety and accessibility for disabled persons are all included.

Standards are defined as international (from an international standards body), European (adopted by a European standards organisation) and national (adopted by a national standards body).

There are also definitions of European technical approval, common technical specifications and technical reference.

All definitions are contained in Annex VI.

Article 23 of the Directive requires standards to be set out in contract notices, contract documents or additional documents (whatever the latter may be). They are specifically required to take account of accessibility for the disabled and design for all users. They are also required not to discriminate against tenderers.

Unless there are legally binding national rules which are compatible with Community law, technical specifications are required to refer in order of preference to national standards transposing European standards, European technical approvals, common technical standards, international standards or other technical reference systems established by European standardisation bodies. Only when no part of this hierarchy exists may national standards, national technical approvals or national technical specifications be invoked. All references are required to be accompanied by the words 'or equivalent'.

As an alternative to the references mentioned in the above paragraph, the technical specification may be a performance specification including environmental considerations provided the performance specification is sufficiently detailed to ensure that the tenderers know what is required. If required, the performance specification may refer to a part of the detailed hierarchy of standards mentioned above. The other possibility is to refer to the standards for some parts of the specification and to the performance for others.

There are further rules which prevent a public sector organisation from rejecting a tender because of apparent failure by the tenderer to conform with the literal wording of the specification requirement if the tenderer can prove by means of a technical dossier from a manufacturer or a test report from a recognised body that the tenderer has in fact complied with the specification.

There are also rules for environmental characteristics as part of a performance specification. Basically European or multinational eco-labels may be used subject to certain safeguards.

There is a rule requiring that specific makes or sources are not specified. This includes specifying specific processes, trade marks, patents, types or specific origin or production if this eliminates or favours certain organisations or their products. If it is exceptionally needed to use any of these methods of specifying a requirement, the words 'or equivalent' must be used.

Public sector organisations are required to make specifications available on request or to refer to documents which are readily available.

It is obvious from the above abbreviated description of the contents of the Directive with respect to specifications that the procedures need to make clear what is and what is not allowed. Readers are advised to study the contents of the Directive carefully before writing these into the procedures.

Variants, subcontracting and conditions for performance of contracts

Variants are optional offers made by a supplier which may not strictly conform with all the technical aspects of a specification but which might still meet a public sector organisation's requirement.

They may be considered if the award of a contract is based on the most economically advantageous tender and if the specification says that variants are permissible and, if so, what the minimum requirements for the variant should be.

It is not permitted to reject variants if accepting them would mean accepting a service contract instead of a supply contract or vice versa.

Public sector organisations may ask in contract documents or be required to ask by the member state for details of the share of a contract which is to be subcontracted and who the subcontractors may be.

Public sector organisations may also specify special conditions about the performance of a contract subject to these being in conformance with Community law. They must be specified in the call for competition or in the specification. The special conditions may include social or environmental concerns.

Obligations relating to taxes, environmental protection, employment protection provisions and working conditions

The body or bodies from which a tenderer may obtain information about these matters may be stated (or required by the member state to be stated) in the contract documents. If this information is supplied, then the public sector organisation has to request tenderers to confirm in their tenders that they have taken these matters into account.

Procedures

The preferred procedures for letting contracts are the open procedure or the restricted procedure. In certain circumstances, a procedure known as 'competitive dialogue' may be used and in other circumstances the negotiated procedure may be used with or without a call for competition by means of a contract notice.

Competitive dialogue

Member states may permit public sector procurement organisations to use competitive dialogue if the contracts to be let are so complex that the open or restricted procedure would prevent their being let. The award criteria which must be used for competitive dialogue is most economically advantageous tender.

A contract notice must be published setting out the needs and requirements of the public sector procurement organisation. There may also be a descriptive document setting out this information and, presumably, the contract notice should refer to this.

Procurement organisations must select suitable candidates, presumably from those responding to the notice, using a series of selection criteria which are described in the Directive. The procurement organisation may then begin a competitive dialogue with the selected candidates. All aspects of the proposed contract may be discussed but there must be equality of treatment and information may not be provided in a discriminatory manner. Proposals made by one candidate may not be revealed by the procurement organisation to another without prior agreement of the first candidate.

Competitive dialogue may take place in successive stages to reduce the number of solutions to be discussed by application of the award criteria previously given in the contract notice or the descriptive document. Either the contract notice or the descriptive document need to make it clear that this process may be adopted.

The dialogue is continued until a solution or solutions is/are identified. The candidates are informed of the closure of the dialogue and they are then asked to make their final tenders on the basis of the solutions proposed during the dialogue. Further clarification, specifying and fine tuning are permissible but not if they mean changes to the basic features of the tender or of the call to tender.

The procurement organisation must assess the tenders by applying the contract award criteria in the manner specified in the Directive. The award criteria must have been previously published in the contract notice or the descriptive document.

The tenderer which has submitted the most economically advantageous tender may be asked by the procurement organisation to clarify certain aspects of the tender provided this does not modify substantial aspects of the tender or call for tender and provided it does not risk distorting competition or cause discrimination.

This is a new process which was not previously available to public sector organisations in earlier Public Sector Directives. Most public sector organisations will want to include it in their procedures. They should, however, take note of the fact that it may only be used when the contractual requirement is so complex that the open or restricted procedure cannot be used. This is not a condition likely to apply to many contracts in the public sector.

Cases justifying use of the negotiated procedure with prior publication of a contract notice

Procurement organisations may negotiate with tenderers about their tenders submitted following a call for competition and, presumably, an invitation to tender in the following cases:

- Only irregular tenders or tenders unacceptable under national provisions compatible with various requirements of the Directive have been received in response to an open, restricted or competitive dialogue invitation. The original terms of the contract must not be substantially altered. Readers are advised to consult the Directive about the precise nature of the requirements which apply to this provision. Although they are wide ranging, it is unlikely that they will apply a great deal in practice. Some provision may be needed in procedures but it is unlikely to be used very much.

- If overall pricing is not possible owing to the nature of the works, supplies or services. This is expected to be unusual.

- If the contract specifications of services *inter alia* services within Category 6 of Annex IIA (financial services: insurance services, banking and investment services) and intellectual services such as services involving the design of works cannot be defined with sufficient provision.

- Works are to be performed solely for the purposes of research, testing and development and not with the aim of ensuring profitability or recovering research and development costs.

The negotiation may take place in successive stages and must be conducted in such a way as to be non-discriminatory.

Cases justifying use of the negotiated procedure without a prior call for competition

The cases are:

1. For public works, supply and service contracts:
    (m) no tenders or no suitable tenders or no applications in response to an open or restricted procedure but the contract which is placed must remain substantially the same as that advertised and a report is sent to the Commission if requested;

(n)   contract can only be undertaken by one supplier because of technical or artistic reasons or for reasons connected with the protection of an exclusive right;

(o)   extreme urgency owing to unforeseeable events not attributable to the procurement organisation and making impossible compliance with the time limits for the open or restricted procedures.

2.   For public supply contracts:

(p)   the products involved are purely for research, experiment, study or development. This does not apply to quantity production to test the commercial viability or to the recovery of research and development costs;

(q)   additional deliveries by the existing supplier which either partially replace normal supplies or installations or are in addition to existing supplies or installations but which are necessarily bought from that supplier owing to compatibility problems provided the length of the contract does not as a general rule exceed three years;

(r)   supplies purchased on commodity markets which quote them;

(s)   purchases of supplies on particularly advantageous terms from organisations which are winding up, going into liquidation, bankrupt, etc.

3.   For public service contracts: the contract is awarded following a design contract organised in accordance with the Directive. If awarded to one of the winners of such a contest, all winners have to be invited to negotiate.

4.   For public works and public service contracts:

   (t)   additional works or services not originally specified but now needed owing to unforeseen circumstances. They have to be awarded to original contractor but only when they cannot be separated from the main works or services without great inconvenience or, if they can be separated, they have to be strictly necessary for the later stages of the contract for the original works or services. The aggregate value of the additional contracts awarded for this reason cannot exceed 50% of the amount of the original contract;

   (u)   new works which are a repetition of existing works provided the 'works or services are in conformity with a basic project for which the original contract was awarded according to the open or restricted procedure'. Notice has to be given that this may be done and the cost of these new works has to be taken into account for aggregation purposes. This is only permissible for a three-year period following conclusion of the original contract.

Framework agreements

Framework agreements are only permissible in the public sector if EU member states allow them to be used. If framework agreements are allowed, then they have to be let in compliance with the Directive; in particular, framework agreements may only be let using the award criteria of lowest price or most economically advantageous tender.

The Directive distinguishes between framework agreements awarded to one supplier and framework agreements to which several suppliers are a party. In the latter case, each of the suppliers can, presumably, supply the same goods or services as specified in the framework agreement as any of the other parties to the framework. In other words, all the suppliers which are party to the framework can supply whatever is specified in the framework.

If the framework is with a number of suppliers, then the minimum number of suppliers is specified in the Directive as being three providing at least three suppliers can satisfy the selection criteria and that at least three admissible tenders meet the award criteria. Presumably, the number may be less than three if only one or two suppliers and their tenders meet these criteria.

When the framework is with a single supplier, call-off orders have to be let in accordance with the terms of the framework but it is permissible for the procurement organisation to consult with the supplier to supplement the supplier's tender. There is no explanation of what 'supplement' means.

When the framework has been concluded with a number of suppliers, then call-off orders may be awarded as specified in the framework agreement without reopening competition or there may be a competition between the suppliers if there are no rules in the framework or if they are insufficient in some way to permit a selection on their basis. In essence, a tendering exercise has to be conducted by the procurement organisation. It has to consult the suppliers about every call-off order to be awarded, presumably to let them know that the business is available and to invite bids. The procurement organisation has to fix a time limit for bids which is sufficiently long to permit the suppliers to bid, receive tenders in writing and keep them confidential until the expiry of the time limit and award the call-off order to the supplier which has submitted the best bid on the basis of the award criteria in the framework agreement. This presumes that there will be award criteria and it would seem that there will now have to be.

Procurement organisations may not amend the terms of the framework agreement when awarding call-off orders and this is particularly applicable if there is only one supplier which is a party to the framework agreement.

Framework agreements may not last longer than four years unless there are exceptional circumstances 'duly justified', particularly by the subject of the framework agreement.

These are modifications to the way in which framework agreements usually operate. In general, the modus operandi of a framework agreement is covered in the framework terms and conditions and not in procurement procedures. For public sector procurement organisations, it would be prudent to have a section in the procedures which deals with frameworks.

Dynamic purchasing systems

A dynamic purchasing system is defined in the Directive as a completely electronic process for making commonly used purchases which meets the needs of the procurement organisation and which is of limited duration and open, while it is available, to any supplier which satisfies the selection criteria and submits an indicative tender which meets the specification. A dynamic purchasing system is possibly some sort of market site, discussed in Chapter 14 dealing with e-procurement.

Member states may permit these to be used. The open procedure has to be used to set up all the contracts procured using a dynamic purchasing system. Suppliers must be admitted to the system if they satisfy the selection criteria and have submitted an indicative tender which meets the specification (presumably the specification has the contents described in the next paragraph) and if they have submitted satisfactory additional documents which may be required. Suppliers have to be permitted to improve their indicative tender at any time provided it continues to comply with the specification.

A procurement organisation must publish a contract notice saying that it is setting up a dynamic purchasing system. It must also give information in the specification about whatever is to be purchased using the dynamic purchasing system and information about the system itself such as the connection arrangements. The specification must be made freely available by electronic means as have any additional documents, and the Internet address where these may be consulted has to be disclosed.

Any supplier must be permitted to submit an indicative tender at any time during the existence of the dynamic purchasing system. The supplier must be freely admitted to the system as described above. Procurement organisations have 15 days from the date of the submission of the indicative tender to complete the evaluation of the tender and the supplier with respect to the selection criteria but this may be extended if no invitation to tender is issued before completion of the evaluation.

The procurement organisation has to notify the supplier as early as possible about its acceptance or rejection as a participant on the system.

Each contract to be let then has to be the subject of an invitation to tender but, before issuing the invitation, the procurement organisation must issue a simplified contract notice inviting an indicative tender from all suppliers. The time limit for submission of the these indicative tenders is 15 days from the date of issue of the simplified contract notice. Formal tendering can only take place after evaluation of the indicative tenders. On the basis of these indicative tenders, the procurement organisation now invites formal tenders to a time limit which it must set. The contract has to be awarded to the supplier submitting the best tender; this is determined by applying the award criteria which have to be listed in the simplified contract notice but which may be described in more detail in the invitation to tender.

A dynamic purchasing system may only last for four years and no payment may be required from suppliers to use it.

If a system of this nature is to be used by the public sector organisation, it should be described in the procedures.

Public works contracts: particular rules on subsidised housing schemes

This is a specialist area and readers are recommended to consult the Directive.

Notices

The procedures will have to describe the notices which need to be placed in order to call for competition. The notices must be sent to the Commission's Office for the Official Publications of the European Communities in a specified format. They may also be published on a buyer profile.

The *prior information notice* is a notice to be published annually for supplies, services and works. For supplies to be bought using a contract or a framework agreement, a prior information notice has to be published if the aggregated value for a product area (obtained by referring to the CPV nomenclature) is equal to or greater than €750,000. The same annual threshold applies to services but only to the categories which appear in Annex XVIIA to which the rules of the Directives apply. The notices for supplies and services have to be sent to the Commission or published on a buyer profile as soon as possible after the start of a budgetary year.

For works and for framework agreements (presumably for works), the annual threshold is the same at €6,242,000 which makes works subject to the Directives anyway. These notices have to be sent to the Commission or published on the buyer profile as soon as possible after the decision approving the planning of the works or framework agreements.

The prior information notice is required for 12 months' requirements looking forward. There are rules about their format and notices published on buyer profiles have to be forwarded electronically to the Commission.

It is possible for procurement organisations to reduce the compulsory periods for tendering provided they have published a prior information notice.

The Directive requires that *contract notices* are published for contracts and framework agreements subject to the Directive. The type of notice depends on whether it is for the open or restricted procedures or the negotiated procedure with a call for competition or a competitive dialogue. Contract notices also have to be issued to set up a dynamic purchasing system and simplified contract notices have to be issued for each contract to be let using the dynamic purchasing system.

Procurement organisations also have to issue notices for the award of a contract or framework agreement within 48 days after the award of a contract or framework agreement. The same is true for contracts let using a dynamic purchasing system although notices may be grouped and published quarterly provided they are published within 48 days of the end of each quarter.

The publication of notices, briefly described above, is a legal requirement and there will have to be rules in the procedures covering this.

Form and manner of publication of notices

The Directive specifies the information to be included in the various notices and says that they might be sent electronically by accessing the preferred format at *http://simap.eu.int* or by other means. If sent electronically using the preferred format, publication is promised within five days of the notice being sent; otherwise it is within 12 days but this can be five days in exceptional circumstances provided the notice is sent by fax.

Notices are published in an official language of the Community and it is the procurement organisation which selects this.

The procedures will need to make it clear that notices cannot be published nationally before the date they are sent to the Commission and national notices cannot contain different information to that sent to the Commission or published on a buyer profile. They have to mention the date of dispatch to the Commission or the date of publication on the buyer profile.

The procedures will also need to make it clear that periodic indicative notices cannot be published on a buyer profile before dispatch to the Commission and again the date of their dispatch must be stated.

It will also be necessary for the procedures to state how the procurement organisation will prove that it has sent the notices to the Commission and how the procurement organisation will deal with the confirmation of publication from the Commission.

Time limits for receipt of requests to participate and for receipt of tenders

The Directive requires the procurement organisation to take account of the complexity of the contract and the time needed to compile a tender. For the open procedure, it sets, for receipt of tenders, a minimum of 52 days from the date on which the contract notice was sent.

For restricted procedures, for negotiated procedures with publication of a contract notice and for competitive dialogue, the minimum period for suppliers to apply to participate is 37 days from the date on which the contract notice was sent. For restricted procedures, suppliers have a minimum of 40 days from the issue of the invitation to tender.

However, the tendering periods of 52 days and 40 days stipulated above may be reduced to 36 days 'but in no circumstances to less than 22 days' if a prior information notice has been issued. Presumably this means that 36 days is preferred but anything down to 22 days is permissible. These reductions only apply if the prior information notice includes all the specified information on the form provided this information was available when the notice was published. The notice must also have been issued for publication at least 52 days to 12 months before the issue of the contract notice.

The time limits for receipt of tenders may be reduced by seven days if the notices have been drawn up and sent electronically as specified at *http://simap.eu.int*.

A reduction of five days is permissible in the time for receipt of tenders if the procurement organisation 'offers unrestricted and full direct access by electronic means to the contract documents and any supplementary documents'. This five days may be added to the seven days mentioned above.

The procedures will have to incorporate these time limits. They will also have to require the period for receipt of tenders to be extended to make good any delay in issuing specifications and supplementary documents in accordance with the open procedure. The Directive requires these to be issued within six days of a request to participate if they are not offered on a freely available electronic system. An extension must also be granted if tenders can only be made after a site visit or after an on-the-spot inspection. Additional information requested by a supplier must also be supplied not later than six days before the date set for receipt of tenders.

For the restricted procedure, the competitive dialogue procedure and the negotiated procedure, any additional information requested by suppliers (most probably clarifications of aspects in the invitation to tender) must be supplied within six days of the request. If this target period is also not met, then the tender period must be extended to compensate fully for that failure.

The Directive also permits shorter periods for request to participate in the event of urgency. These only apply to restricted and negotiated procedures and if it is impractical to meet the time limits mentioned above. The time limits are ten days if the contract notice was sent electronically and 15 days otherwise. In similar circumstances, the time limit for tendering for the restricted procedure is ten days.

Open procedures: specifications, additional documents and information

These have been largely addressed in the previous section.

Invitations to submit a tender, participate in the dialogue or negotiate

The requirements here are not dissimilar to those described in this book for issuing tenders but the following should be included in any procedures. Invitations to tender have to be issued simultaneously and in writing, include the specifications or say how, by when and from where they can be obtained and what fee is payable. Additional information if requested by suppliers should be issued no later than six days before the date for submission of tenders (but note, as mentioned above, the extension of the tender period if there is a delay in issuing this information).

The invitation to tender must contain a reference to the contract notice, the date when the tenders are due (in the case of competitive dialogue, this has to appear in the invitation to tender and not in the invitation to participate in a dialogue), the address to which they must be sent, the language or languages to be used, a reference to any 'possible adjoining documents' (see the Directive for more details of this) and the contract award criteria and their relative importance or weighting in descending order, but only if they are not given in the contract notice or the specification or the descriptive document.

If a competitive dialogue is to be used, the following must be included: the date when the dialogue is to start, the address where it is to be conducted and the language or languages to be used.

Informing candidates and tenderers

This requires procurement organisations to advise in writing candidates and tenderers, i.e. suppliers, as soon as possible of their decision to award a contract, to place a framework agreement or to admit to a dynamic purchasing system. Suppliers also have to be informed of any decisions not to award a contract or place a framework agreement. Similarly, any decision to recommence a procedure or to implement a dynamic purchasing system must also be advised.

On inquiry, unsuccessful candidates have to be told why they were unsuccessful. Rejected tenderers have to be told of the characteristics and relative advantages of the selected tender plus the name of the successful tenderer or the names of parties to a framework agreement.

All of this has to be done within 15 days of a written request.

Under certain circumstances, some information may be withheld. The circumstances are when disclosure would impede law enforcement, be contrary to the public interest, prejudice the legitimate commercial concerns of suppliers or prejudice fair competition.

Much of these requirements are similar to what has already been recommended elsewhere in this book for inclusion in the procedures. Readers in the public sector should only need to make some modifications to more nearly meet the requirements of the Directive.

Rules applicable to communication

This section contains rules about the use of post, fax, telephone and electronic means of communication. None of these means must be chosen to restrict participation by potential suppliers. Confidentiality and integrity of data must be preserved. Requests by suppliers to participate may be made by telephone, in which case they must be confirmed in writing. Provided it is necessary for the purposes of legal proof, procurement organisations may require in the contract notice that suppliers send confirmation by post or by electronic means of any request to participate made by fax.

Content of reports

For every contract, framework agreement and dynamic purchasing system, the Directive requires procurement organisations to produce a written report giving details about the organisation itself, the subject matter of the contract, framework etc., the name(s) of successful suppliers selected to participate, the reasons for their selection, the names of those rejected from participation, the reasons for their rejection, the reason(s) for rejecting abnormally low tenders, the name of the supplier(s) which won the business, the reasons for their success, how much they intend to subcontract if this is known, justification of the use of a negotiated procedure and the circumstances for using competitive dialogue. Alternatively, if it has been decided to award no contract, the reasons for this decision must be given.

This report has to be communicated to the Commission if requested. However, it is probably prudent to produce the report when the information is still fresh in the procurement agent's mind rather than try and find it when asked, possibly after some considerable lapse of time. For this reason, the procedures will need to deal with this question.

Verification of the suitability and choice of participants and award of contracts

Procurement organisations may reduce the number of tenderers to a minimum of five if using the restricted procedure and to a minimum of three if using either the negotiated procedure with a call for competition or the competitive dialogue procedure. Non-discriminatory rules and criteria must be used to make the selection and these must be declared in the contract notice. If there are less than the minimum numbers of tenderers available, then only those tenderers which responded to the contract notice and which meet the rules and criteria may be invited to participate.

This approach is not dissimilar to qualification described in this book.

Personal situation of the candidate or tenderer

The procedures will need to stipulate the following reasons permitted by the Directive for excluding an organisation from participating: participation in a criminal organisation, corruption, fraud, money laundering.

Further reasons for exclusion include various forms of financial instability, an offence concerning professional misconduct, failure to meet obligations relating to the payment of social security or taxes, and serious misrepresentation.

All of these are defined in the Directive and the reader should consult the Directive for more information.

The Directive provides for evidence that an organisation is not guilty of any of the above: basically provision of a judicial record or equivalent or a declaration made on oath or before some competent authority.

The important thing which the procedures must make clear is that the right to restrict suppliers from participating is defined and limited. Readers should consult the Directive for the detail.

Suitability to pursue the professional activity

This deals with registration of suppliers on professional or trade registers in their home country. Procurement organisations are permitted to ask for proof of this if it is a requirement in the procurement organisation's member state that a supplier has this qualification.

This is likely to have limited applicability and might not be needed in the procedures. Readers should again check the detail in the Directive.

Economic and financial standing

This concerns financial checks on a potential supplier and limits the checks to one or more of the following: appropriate bank statements or professional indemnity insurance, balance sheets and information about the overall turnover and, if appropriate, the turnover over the last three years in the area covered by the contract.

The supplier may rely on the financial capabilities of other organisations with which it has links but it must then prove that these resources are available.

If, for valid reasons, the tenderer can produce none of the above proof, other means of proof may be offered provided the procurement organisation considers these to be appropriate.

There will probably be a need to describe these limitations in the procedures because the exact way in which the procurement organisation wishes to check the economic and financial standing has to be specified in the contract notice or invitation to tender.

Technical and/or professional ability

The Directive specifies how a procurement organisation may check the technical and/or professional ability of an organisation. These will have to be included in the procedures to ensure compliance with the Directive. They are:

- a list of works carried out over the last five years with certificates of satisfactory completion of the most important – various details are given in the Directive and must be shown on the certificates;

- a list of principal deliveries of supplies or main services provided over the past three years – the Directive gives details about the composition of these lists;

- information provided by technicians or technical bodies – again there is more detail in the Directive;

- a description of the supplier's technical facilities and measures;

- a check of the supplier's production/technical capacities depending on whether it is supplies or services, and on the quality control measures and study and research facilities, but only if the supplies or services are complex;

- educational and professional qualifications of personnel;

- in appropriate circumstances for works and services, the supplier's environmental management measures;

- average manpower over the last three years for a service provider and a works contractor;

- a service provider's or a works contractor's tools, plant or technical equipment;

- the proportion of a contract which a service provider intends to subcontract;

- for supplies: samples, descriptions and/or photographs, certificates produced by a competent quality control body attesting conformity to specifications or standards.

The procurement organisation has to say in the contract notice or the invitation to tender which of the above will be applied.

If a supplier wishes, it may rely on the capabilities of another entity or entities with which it has links but it may be asked to prove that these capabilities are available to it.

If siting or installation of supplies is required or if the contract is to be for services and/or works then the procurement organisation may evaluate the supplier's skills, efficiency, experience and reliability.

The above have a material bearing on supplier selection and there will be a need to incorporate them into the procedures.

Quality assurance standards, environmental management standards and additional documentation and information

These three clauses set the standard which may be specified for quality assurance and environmental management. They specify what may be acceptable and which organisations may do any certification or attestation work.

For procurement organisations for which these standards are important, there will need to be a reference in the procedures.

Official lists of approved economic operators and certification by bodies established under public and private law

This article deals with official listing by member states of suppliers, service providers and works contractors. Much of it is addressed to the member states about how they should do the registration/listing. Suppliers etc. are entitled to submit a registration certificate but these do not mean that the supplier will meet the required standards for many of the matters discussed above, although information which can be deduced from the registration certificate may not be questioned.

This is a fairly complicated area and reference to the Directive is advised to see whether it is likely to apply to an organisation's procurement. If it is, then inclusion in the procedures might be advisable.

Contract award criteria

This article limits the criteria for evaluation of a tender to lowest price or most economically advantageous tender. If the latter is to be used, the component criteria must be scored and weighted and these have to be specified in the contract notice or the contract documents or in the descriptive document for competitive dialogue. This statement can be a range with an appropriate maximum spread.

If weighting is not possible, then the descending order of importance of the component criteria must be stated.

This aspect should be included in the procedures.

Electronic auctions

Electronic auctions may be permitted by member states. Procurement organisations must advise in the contract notice of their intention to hold an electronic auction. This must state what quantifiable values (usually money) the supplier will be bidding in the auction, what limits are to be applied to these values, what information will be made available to suppliers during the auction, information about the auction process, the conditions for bidding including any minimum differences and any relevant information about the equipment and connections.

All of this is fairly straightforward and the procedures would need to reflect the same.

Procurement organisations are required to make a full initial evaluation of any tenders in accordance with the award criteria and their weightings. This presumably refers to all those aspects which will not be bid in the electronic auction. Those suppliers which have submitted admissible bids must be invited to participate in the auction.

The invitation has to contain all the information to enable participants to do so. If the most economically advantageous tender is to be used for evaluation, then the invitation has to give the full outcome of the evaluation. It also has to state the mathematical formula which will be used in the auction 'to determine the automatic re-rankings on the basis of the new prices and/or values submitted'. This formula has to incorporate all the weightings for the most economically advantageous tender analysis and a separate formula has to be provided for each variant.

The auction system has to instantaneously communicate to suppliers engaged in bidding sufficient information for them to ascertain their rankings. Most auction systems do this. The identities of the participants may not be revealed.

Three ways in which an auction may be closed are listed: at a predetermined date stipulated in the invitation to take part in the auction, when there are no new bids provided the time which will be allowed to elapse after the last bid has been stated in the invitation or when the number of phases in the auction has been completed provided this number was defined in the invitation and the close-out time for each phase was given.

Much of this is about the auction process and would need to be built into the auction system. However, the need to include the relevant information in an invitation is something which should be included in the procedures.

The auction may not start earlier than two working days after the invitation was sent out. The auction may be conducted in successive phases.

Abnormally low tenders

This part of the Directive requires procurement organisations to query abnormally low tenders before rejecting them. It is also prudent to query them before accepting them.

The procurement organisation is required to ask for more detail about the constituent parts of a tender, in particular about construction methods, manufacturing methods or the services to be provided, about the technical solutions to be chosen or any exceptionally favourable conditions which might be applicable, about the originality of the work, supplies or services to be provided, about compliance with employment protection or working conditions requirements and about whether the supplier is receiving state aid.

If the supplier has received state aid, the tender can only be rejected if the supplier cannot prove that the aid is legal. If the procurement organisation rejects a bid on the grounds of illegal state aid, it must inform the Commission of the European Union.

Checking to verify an abnormally low tender is good practice and has been addressed in this book. Procurement organisations in the public sector will need to take account of these requirements when drafting that section.

The remainder of the Public Sector Directive

The remainder of the Directive deals with:

- public works concessions;

- design contests;

- statistical obligations, executory powers and final provisions.

These are issues not normally dealt with in procurement procedures and the reader is referred to the Directive for guidance.